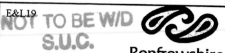

THE ISLANDS SERIES

† The Aran Islands
  The Isle of Arran
*Corsica
*Canary Islands: Fuerteventura
*The Falkland Islands
*Grand Bahama
†The Isle of Mull
  Lundy
  The Maltese Islands
†Orkney
  St. Kilda and other Hebridean Outliers
‡*The Seychelles
  †Shetland
‡*Singapore
‡*The Solomon Islands
  *Vancouver Island

in preparation
  Achill
  Bermuda
  The Island of Bute
  Cyprus
  Gotland
  Puerto Rico
  Skye
  St Helena
  Tobago

* Published in the United States by Stackpole
† Published in the United States by David & Charles
‡ Distributed in Australia by Wren Publishing Pty Ltd Melbourne

HARRIS AND
LEWIS
Outer Hebrides

by FRANCIS THOMPSON

DAVID & CHARLES

NEWTON ABBOT

0 7153 5983 5

First published 1968
Revised edition 1973

© Francis Thompson 1968, 1973

Printed in Great Britain by
Redwood Press Limited Trowbridge Wiltshire
for David & Charles (Holdings) Limited
South Devon House Newton Abbot Devon

To my wife, Margaret

CONTENTS

HARRIS AND LEWIS

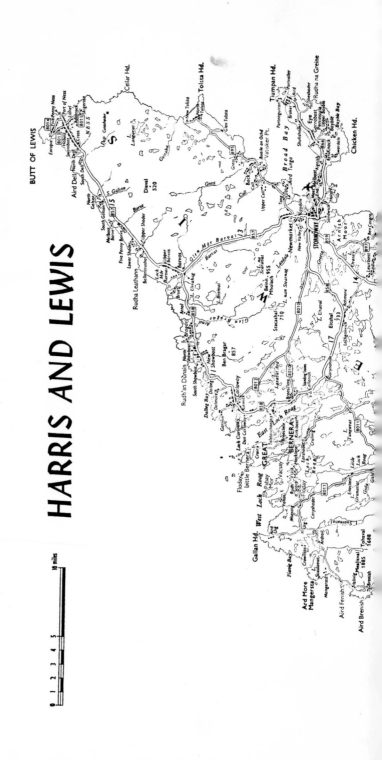

ILLUSTRATIONS

ILLUSTRATIONS

*The author wishes to thank his wife for the
illustrations on pages 33, 38, 102, 141, 170.*

1   INTRODUCTION

THOUGH generally referred to as separate islands, Harris and Lewis are geographically speaking one island—the largest landmass in the Outer Hebrides. Its latitude is approximately 57° 40′ to 58° 40′ N; its longitude 6° to 7° W. Many have expressed surprise at the size of the island, which is over 800 square miles in extent. From top to bottom the crow's-flight distance is just over 80 miles, and from east to west about 14 miles. By road, however, the north-south journey (the Butt of Lewis to Rodel in Harris) is a good 80 miles. And by road from east to west (Tiumpan Head lighthouse to Breinish in Uig) is 54 miles.

Among the oldest islands of the world Harris and Lewis is founded, like a strong resisting house, on rock, on gneiss said to be the oldest fragment of Europe. From a distance the tough durable Lewisian gneiss is easily recognisable as bare, barren, elongated domes and ridges, giving a hummocky appearance to the landscape. Among other rock types to be found is a patch of a few hundred acres of granite in the parish of Barvas, on the west side of Lewis; some torridonian sandstone showing on each side of Broad Bay, around Stornoway; and the tertiary basalt of the Shiant Isles. These latter islands, pin-points of high land, are geologically speaking insular outliers of Skye, though they are but a few miles or so off the Lewis coastline. Another set of islands, associated with Harris and Lewis, are the St Kildas, composed of gabbros and basalt.

The continual exposure of the rocks on the island makes it easy for those interested in geology to see just what happened those countless years ago. Sands, muds and limestones were formed in an ancient sea, to be later heated and recrystallised as volcanic eruptions occurred. During this boiling, a seasoning touch of molten granite was added. Later, still in an ancient season, the rocks were thrust up and crushed against each other to form today's geological spectacular. Dark-coloured horneblende and

13

mica-sparkled gneiss show the intense shearing. And crushed rock, known as flinty crush because it splinters so easily, adds another sight for the modern eye. The Stornoway beds, as they are called, are broadly known as torridonian sandstone, old red sandstone, or triassic; some geologists regard them as part of the pre-Cambrian torridonian series.

From geological evidence, twice did vast icesheets move over the rock-faces to round off the sharp corners of the island. And, as individually then as now, geologists think that there may have been a third small glaciation—a private Hebridean one. Today, the scenery bears the imprint of glacial striae or scratchings. Polished rocks show scores; lochs are gravel-damned, and there are countless small lochans and tarns formed from deep gougings in solid rock. There is some evidence too of a depression or land-sinking during a much later post-glacial time. Many times have fishermen found, far below the present high-water line, stumps of trees and buried submarine peat, the wasting remains of former land vegetation. Martin Martin, who wrote of the Western Isles about 1695, said of Berneray, one of the small islands in the Sound of Harris: 'The west end of this island which looks to St Kilda, is called the wooden harbour, because the sands at low water discover several trees that have formerly grown there. Sir Norman MacLeod told me that he had seen a tree cut there, which was afterwards made into a harrow.' These vegetation remains indicate a former fertility. Volcanic action and deposit, the makings of good soil were, however, largely carried away by glacial movement to leave a thin scraping of boulder clay clinging to the base rock for dear life.

Lewis is largely rolling moors of blanket peat with many lochs and rivers. To the west of Lewis, in Uig, high hills begin to raise the eye. In North Harris, the hills are higher, reaching their peak in the Clisham (2,622 ft above sea level). These are not strictly speaking mountains. But they do present not a few problems to climbers, having some formidable rock-faces, and on the seaward side are virtually unscaleable cliffs. Much of the ice-moulded landscape of South Harris is rocky and barren, gneiss outcrops cover many acres in places, and are almost completely devoid of any kind of vegetation, except where, in the odd crevice, like lurking thieves, patches of heather, deer-grasses or moorland plants live as they can on thin layers of peaty soil. To relieve the hard scenery there are, on sunny days, glintings of water, lochs or rivers flowing uneasily over beds of primordial rock.

Area (in acres)

	Land	Inland water	Saltmarsh	Foreshore	Tidal water	TOTAL
Harris	123,752	3,110	—	6212	105	133,178
Lewis	404,184	24,863	230	7775	150	437,200
						570,378

PEAT AND RIVERS

The peat overlays of the island are reckoned to be not much more than 7,000 years old. To strengthen this figure, when the megalithic circle of Callernish, on the west of Lewis, was excavated by Sir James Matheson in 1857-8, a depth of 5 ft of peat was removed to expose the giant stones. Only the tops of these stones were showing before excavation was begun; the resultant calculation confirmed the age of this infertile blanket. Peat is decomposed organic matter without the sweetening of lime. The resulting material is sour, and highly acid in character, which checks the bacterial action necessary for good soil to be made. With compaction and age, peat becomes colloidal in texture, with a water content of about 92 per cent. Peat is still being formed in Lewis, though its progress is imperceptibly slow.

Frequent diggings have uncovered evidence that the island was once densely wooded. The remains of trees, and the bones of certain animals and birds associated with savannah and woodland, add point to this. Under the blanket of peat lies what is called boulder clay, glacially deposited on the gneiss rock; many acres of this clay have been exposed through centuries of digging up peat for fuel. Such skinned ground is called *gearraidh*, and it forms the basis of a soil which, when worked together with shell sand and seaweed, becomes quite fertile. Of natural soil, so much taken for granted in richer places in Britain, there are a few patches in Lewis, at Garrabost and Ness; the valley of Strond, near Rodel in Harris, has much strong red loam.

INTRODUCTION

One glance at an island map will show how numerous are the lochs. These and the short rivers and streams do their best to drain the rainwater which averages about 45 inches, with an added 10 inches or so for precipitation in the form of very fine rain or mist. That the rockbase of the island is much like an impervious saucer which overflows easily is seen shortly after a heavy rainfall. Streams and rivers become torrents of brown, foam-flecked waters tumbling to the sea or to some nearby loch. The watershed of Lewis runs from north-east to south-west, keeping about the middle of the island, except in the north where it approaches the eastern side. The rivers, all quite short, have at one time in their history carried good stocks of trout and salmon; some still do. The Grimersta River, though less than two miles long, is reckoned to be the best salmon river in Europe. Its waters come from the great loch and catchment area of Loch Langavat (Norse : Long Water). The River Creed, just outside Stornoway, is also known for its salmon which, in the right season of year, can be seen a tantalising arm's length away, making their way up river. Another salmon river is that beside Amhuinnsuidhe Castle in North Harris, where the salmon leap several feet over a sheer rockface to gain the upper waters. Of the lochs, virtually all abounding with trout, the largest is Loch Langavat, about six miles in length.

FLORA

The first reaction of the visitor to the island is to comment on the scarcity of trees. 'Treeless' is a relative term, however, for there *are* trees on the island. And the island was not always so bare. After the last Ice Age retreated some thirteen milleniums ago, the initial tundra was covered by birch scrub which developed into a wide birch-pine forest with some dense hazel undergrowth. Oak, alder, birch, pine, ash and rowan could be found. Then, with the advent of the cool, wet, sub-Atlantic period about 3,000 years ago, conditions became ideal for the formation of blanket bog and the accumulation of peat. The trees failed and fell; natural clearings formed. When the Norsemen visited the Hebrides, they found substantial areas of woodland, deteriorating, but still sufficient to attract their attention.

(*above*) A typical coast scene on the island: the beach at Mangersta, on the
west of Lewis

(*below*) Land scene at Timsgarry, Uig, Lewis

(*above*) The car ferry *Hebrides*, at Tarbert Pier, Harris

(*below*) The interior of St Clement's Church, Rodel, Harris, showing the carved tomb of Alasdair Crotach, a MacLeod of Dunvegan (d c 1547)

Pursuing a 'scorched-earth' policy, a Norse leader, Magnus Bare-leg, on a punitive expedition to Lewis in 1098 destroyed much of the island's natural surface resources. Trees were a particular target. Following this wanton destruction, the shrinkage of wooded areas in the island was accelerated by the requirements of the population and by the developing peat. Captain Dymes, an Englishman who visited Lewis in 1630 in connection with Charles I's fishery schemes, reported 'there are many eagles and hawks in the isle which breed in the clefts of rocks, for this place is so destitute of wood that there is not one tree growing in the whole island.' Martin Martin almost confirmed this a generation later : 'I saw big roots of trees at the head of Loch Erisort, and there is about a hundred young birch and hazel trees on the southwest side of Loch Stornoway, but there is no more wood on the island.' Before Sir James and Lady Matheson came to Lewis in 1844, the MacKenzie gardens outside the old Seaforth Lodge, where Lews Castle now stands, had many fruiting apple trees.

The mention in 1695 of the Stornoway plantation is interesting, for it is here that today stands the greatest concentration of trees in the whole of the Hebrides, in the grounds of Lews Castle. Some 300 acres of trees here, mostly conifers, but with some hardwoods and deciduous trees, were planted by Lady Matheson about a century ago. Soil had to be transported from the mainland to supplement the scanty layer of peat which overlay the hard Lewis rock. Another of Lady Matheson's legacies is a small area at Achmore, one of the few townships to be found inland, far from the sea. Here, larch and other conifers grew well and would be there today had not a fierce gale blown them down in 1921. There are some ninety-year-old Corsican pines at the head of Little Loch Roag. Another plantation of deciduous and coniferous trees can be found at Grimersta on the Atlantic coast of Lewis, and two more small areas of trees are at Scalisgro, on the east side of Lewis, and in Glen Valtos. In Harris, there are some magnificent sycamores at Tarbert; and at Borve, on the west side of the island, are several acres of stunted mountain pines. In addition, dwarf rowans cover many tiny islands in the lochs.

Natural tree growth is impossible in most areas because of the peat. The strong and frequent winds are also a deterrent. The isopeths of average wind-speed show an overall figure of 17·5 mph. Winds of gale force (8 or more on the Beaufort Scale) occur in Stornoway about twenty times a year, and blow for an annual average of about 378 hours, loosening trees from the shallow ground and stunting growth. Yet another factor is the fine salt spray, 'small rain with salt in it from the sea', which is carried far inland over the island, the prevailing winds blowing straight off the Atlantic Ocean in a south-westerly to westerly direction.

The flora of Harris and Lewis merits a full volume on its own. Far from being sterile, the moors, the hills, the machar-lands, the islets in the lochs, all present subjects of great interest. To the botanist, the island is a region of moorland with loch, marsh, bog, burn and high hills, with sometimes extensive patches of the old man's skin protruding to show the Lewisian gneiss. Variation is offered by the addition of rocky hill-slopes, fine sea-cliffs and shingly bays; sandy parts add to the floral variety, richest in the marine outreaches. To catalogue the flora is to list names which can be appreciated only by seeing the plants themselves in the habitat which they have taken as their own, much as the Hebridean *homo sapiens* has taken to himself the 'savage' country which awed early tourists. Rare species have been found by visiting botanists, and are discussed in the work of Professor Heslop Harrison and his group from Durham University. There is colour aplenty at all seasons of the year in the island; one merely needs to train the eye to look for it, to find, for example, those miniature woodlands in such places as the gorge of the river Amhuinn Gillan Tallair, in south Harris. And in particular, one might mention the blaze of whins around Stornoway; the luxuriant wild growth on the sandy machar-lands in Uig; just north of Stornoway, and at Ness; the miniature sieges of growth on the lochs' islands; and the Alpine plants associated with the higher reaches of land in Uig and North Harris.

Whereas the land is a relatively poor place, the sea is rich, and so is the flora and bird-life to be found round its shores. Near the shore line the grass has a sweet taste liked by sheep. Much of the flora is typical of the island, suited to withstanding the lack of humus to act as a sponge for water, and the paucity of soil for roots. Marram grass, scurvy grass, sea pink, sea campion, thrift and pearlwort are all to be found. It is not often that a plant is given some measure of authority over the affairs of man : but the marram grass—known as 'bent', but not to be confused with the grass botanically referred to as bent *(Agrostis sp)*—is vital in stabilising the sand of the machar-lands; unless grazed or cut, with its dense network of roots it anchors the sand in perpetuity. With the marram, the sea-sedge works hard to form a green coverlet over the sand, and acts as host to other plants, the shell-sand grassland offering excellent grazing for crofters' stock.

The richness of the flora of the macharland has been sung many times, and little wonder. It holds a multitude of what can be called plebian plants such as ragwort, buttercup, daisy, kidney vetch, bird's-foot trefoil, tufted vetch, gentian and primrose. Unfortunately the heavy grazing of these stretches of land results in many plants never being given the opportunity to develop and flower for the plentiful propagation of their species.

FAUNA

The entomologist will also find much of interest. The Hebrides have their own bumble-bee *(Bombus jonellus* var. *hebridensis)*, found nowhere else in the world. Other insects too have found an insular form, adding their rich thread to the weave of natural history in the region : the Dark Green Fritillary butterfly and the Green-veined White. Moths there are in abundance, some such as the Gray Dagger perhaps indicating the existence of woodland conditions in a past time. The abundance of lochs, streams and marshy grounds gives an abundance of dragon-flies and caddis-flies, eight species of which are represented.

Of wild animal life, however, the list is short, due to lack of shelter and poor ground. The red deer is found in the hilly fastnesses of Harris and the Park district of Lewis, though the deer are small, and well poached as one might expect where the density of human population is high. The pine marten, until the 1810s, lived in the region near the Clisham. A rare bat, the pipistrelle, has been found at Rodel. Rats, mice, rabbits, hares and otters are of course to be found.

The interior of the island is poor in bird life, but round the coasts there is a wonderful richness—one might well spend an hour or so with J. A. Harvie-Brown's *A Fauna of the Outer Hebrides*. The Hebrides area is one of the twelve faunal regions of Scotland, and is becoming increasingly the spotting-ground for amateur and professional ornithologists. They see birds such as the skua and red-necked phalarope, breeding at the southernmost limits of their range. The golden eagle, corncrake and redthroated diver, though found in other parts of Scotland, are more plentiful in the region because of the low incidence of human interference; buzzard, merlin and peregrine falcon are also found. Many birds are peculiar to the area: there are Hebridean subspecies of twite, dunnock, song-thrush and wren. Since 1962 the blue tit has begun to colonise the Stornoway woods. And 1960 saw the first arrival of the collared dove, an incomer which, like many a human, has taken a liking to the place and settled down to establish its flourishing community. On Gallows Hill, a low rising overlooking Stornoway, is a large rookery; rooks first reached the island in 1893. Jackdaws arrived at the turn of the century and are now quite numerous. As might be expected, the adjacent harbour and foreshore of Stornoway provide a suitable area for purple sandpipers, turnstone, heron and redshank. Gulls abound. The estuary area just north of Stornoway is the haunt of widgeon, shellduck and teal, among many other birds; a ruff was seen there in 1956. Melbost beach has the largest ternery in the islands, with arctic, common and little terns sharing life together.

The birds on the shore line are mostly waders, divers, ducks and seabirds. Cormorant, shag, gannet, fulmar, arctic skua, terns, gulls of all kinds and oyster-catchers can be found. The full variety of the island's bird life can be seen by visiting not only those sloping lands to the sea, but the cliff-tops, which often have their own numerous bird colonies. The sea's edge, with the push-pull tides, is indeed another area with abundant life of all kinds. Bladderwrack *(fucus vesiculosus)* and knotted wrack *(ascophyllum nodosum)* are there in great quantity, the latter now a significant factor in seaweed-processing activities (Chapter 6). From time immemorial, seaweeds have been a natural resource in the island's economy, used as manure to supply the necessary element of organic matter to keep the land in good heart. Keeping the seaweeds company are the whelks, razor-fish, limpets and mussels, winkles and barnacles, many once used for food, but now left to grow in great numbers, to the delight of seabirds.

For anyone who wishes to have a full list of the richness of fishes found in the inshore waters of the island, there is the Harvie-Brown and Buckley volume (1888) in the *Vertebrate Fauna of Scotland* series. Of the ocean fauna, most famous of course are the common and the grey or Atlantic seals, the latter being one of the largest and most robust of British mammals. A great breeding place for the common seal is the island of Shillay, which lies a mile or two from Pabbay, off the western end of the Sound of Harris. All the island's outliers, North Rona, Sulasgeir and the Shiants, afford a place for breeding. The basking shark, the porpoise, and the blue shark are among other large creatures that frequently haunt Hebridean sea-waters.

LAND WEALTH

In minerals the island is poor. Feldspar was quarried in Harris during the second world war, but it is doubtful whether the workings were economic. The feldspar quarries opened at Lingerbay and Northton in South Harris in 1941 employed some sixty men, the material being sent from Leverburgh for use in the Staffordshire Potteries, for the manufacture of porcelain insulators. The high-grade mineral found in Scandinavia, and the better transport facilities there, led to the close-down of the Harris quarries. At Lingerbay, however, a small quarry yields anorthosite, a white granite used as an abrasive for cleaning products. A recent survey discovered deposits of asbestos on the island of Scarp to the west of Harris.

For some reason there has been, through the centuries, a belief in the mineral wealth of Lewis. As far back as 1616 the records of the Privy Council show an entry: 'Ane patent ardanit to be past to Archibald Prymrois of the copper and lead mynes in Ila, Sky and Lewis.' The Fife Adventurers and the last Lord Seaforth were also optimistic. Lord Seaforth went so far as to commission a survey on the resources of the island by a mineralogist, the Rev James Headrick, in 1800. Nothing much followed Mr

Headrick's recommendations. However, he promised to make experiments on the economic value of the 'bog-ore of iron' found in many parts of the island, with a view to making bar-iron. Peat was to be used as a fuel for smelting.

With so much water on the island, it is natural to expect to find some of it harnessed for the generation of electricity. The Gisla hydro-electric scheme is on the west of Lewis, to the west of the shores of Little Loch Roag. The Harris scheme is at Loch Chliostair, at the foot of the three peaks of Tirgamore (2,227 ft), Ullaval (2,135), and Oreval (2,165). Some 12 per cent of the island's total electricity production is generated thus, the remainder being diesel generation at Stornoway (see Chapter 11).

Next to water, the island's most readily available resource is its stifling blanket of peat, which covers more than 80 per cent of Lewis's land area. It has had a more than significant effect on the natural history of the area, its scenery and the human element. When the deposits were examined in varying detail in 1910-11, it was estimated that they covered no less than 230 square miles, in depths up to 16·5 ft; the average depth of peat over the whole island was assessed at 5 ft. On this basis the deposits would contain approximately 85 million tons of solids. A survey carried out by the Peat Section of the Department of Agriculture & Fisheries for Scotland in 1952 indicated that the earlier estimates were slightly high.

In 1946-7 the Ministry of Fuel & Power reconnoitred the peat deposits on both sides of the Stornoway-Barvas road and indicated that these were suitable for large-scale utilisation. Yet today, despite these Government-backed investigations, the peat deposits of Lewis are still used only for domestic fuel. One of the points made in a 1952 survey was that the area was generally firm enough to take the weight of various bog machines for digging and milling. Another point was that the calorific values of ten out of twelve peat samples were in excess of 10,000 BTU/lb.

CLIMATE

The rainfall has already been mentioned, averaging an annual 43 inches, according to readings taken at the Meteorological

Station of the Air Ministry at Stornoway Airport. About 45 per
cent of the rain falls during the months of April to September in-
clusive. The annual average of days without rain is about 122,
so that some rain is expected on two days out of every three.
May to August is of course the driest period, averaging about fourteen rainless days. The sunshine record shows more sun on the
east coast than on the west, as one might expect. The annual

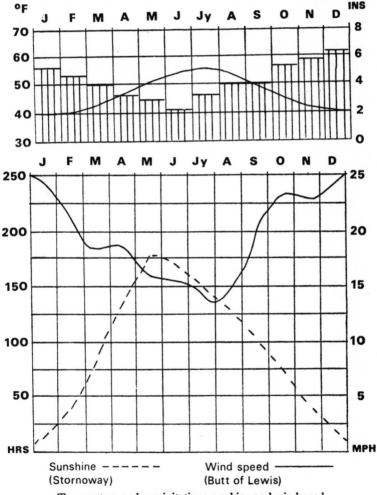

Sunshine – – – – – –   Wind speed ————
(Stornoway)   (Butt of Lewis)

Temperature and precipitation; sunshine and windspeed

average of hours of sunshine is only 1,100 to 1,200, the long-term monthly average of sunshine hours for Stornoway being; May, 195; June, 173; July, 128; August, 133; September, 111. Reducing temperatures quoted to a mean sea level, the range is about 8° C (55° F), from the mean of 6° C (44° F) in January. This January mean is relatively high—compared with the 3° C (38° F) for Cambridge, some several hundred miles farther south—and is due to the body of warm Atlantic water which originates in the Gulf of Mexico. The winter isotherm trend is north to south, emphasising the predominant influence of the Atlantic Ocean as a source of comparative warmth. Snow lies on an annual mean of five mornings each year (Paisley, 10; Edinburgh, 10; Nairn, 20). Also, summer temperatures are lower than those of the south of Scotland and of England. There are, however, much longer hours of summer daylight, a feature of high latitudes.

2 ECOLOGY AND PHYSICAL ENVIRONMENT

THE population of the island huddles round the coastline as round a central hearth. This is mainly because the inland parts of the island are either barren, as in Harris, or infertile bog, as in Lewis. Much of the south Hebrides has, on the west coast, the extremely fertile macharland, but Harris and Lewis do not have these useful patches. The macharland is land built on shell sand and dressed with fertilizing seaweed; it forms a fertile fringe, no more than a belt of varying width between the sea and the acid peat bog on the inland side. Where this land does occur, mainly on the west coast of the island, townships crowd round it for the good growing it can give. The other reason for the attraction of the coast is the obvious one : the close proximity, on the doorstep, of a change of diet, shellfish and inshore fish such as whiting, cod, haddock and mackerel. The exceptions to this coastal grouping are Achmore, Cliascro, and Lochganvich in Lewis.

There is a great physiographical difference between the east and west coasts of the island, this apart from the incidence of macharland on the west coast. The eastern side is steeper to the sea; though sheer cliffs occur at Gallan Head, West Loch Roag. The south-western coastline has high, almost sheer cliffs with few inlets or sheltered harbourages excepting Loch Roag, a magnificent inlet, sheltered at its farthest inland penetration by Great Bernera. The coast on this island side often presents rocky teeth to the Atlantic's buffeting; and often suddenly falls down to sea level to display wide stretches of sand. Uig Bay, where the Red River runs into the sea, is a breath-taking sweep of whiteness. The eastern coast is generally rocky but has more inlets, lochs which carry townships mainly engaged in fishing or tweed manufacture.

ECOLOGY AND PHYSICAL ENVIRONMENT

The crofting township is not quite akin to the English or Lowland village. Primarily it is a collection of dwellings of families who, as social units, gain their subsistence from the land surrounding the houses. The smallest number for a township is four family units. A functional unit of four men was the minimum necessary for a boat crew, or for the teamwork necessary to cultivate land; co-operation was essential if all four families were to survive. And from this grew the same spirit of communal work which in Lewis is seen at its best in the efforts to reclaim peat bog and turn it into fertile grassland.

Hebridean townships come close to being the nearest approach to a classless society. The shape of a township is largely dictated by the nature of the surrounding land. The shape of most of those in Harris and in Lewis is either scattered or linear (houses disposed in line at varying distances from each other), with little natural cover, either plantation or scrub. Often the main road runs through the township; some have begun to develop lateral roads, to give, from the air, the appearance of planning on a grid system. Where gardens are cultivated, the produce tends to be a summer vegetable supply for the household, little if any finding its way to Stornoway shops for sale. Peat is the usual fuel, though in townships near to the centres of Tarbert and Stornoway coal is burned; the cost of freight, however, makes it expensive.

Most of the townships are owned by commercial companies; individual lairds own some five dozen; the remainder belong to public bodies and trusts. The actual distribution of ownership of land on the island is as follows. Harris is virtually owned by individual lairds; a small percentage is owned by commercial companies. The Lochs region of Lewis has a mixed ownership: commercial companies, lairds, and public trust, the former being the largest. Stornoway parish is wholly owned by public trust. The Ness district is virtually the property of commercial companies; a small fraction belongs to public trust. The Uig district is the same, the smaller proportion, less than 10 per cent, being the concern of an individual laird.

In Lewis, the public body mentioned is the Stornoway Trust,

the only one of its kind in the Highlands: when Lewis was sold by Lord Leverhulme in 1923, the parish of Stornoway Landward was given to the townspeople who, in effect, became shareholders in the trust, formed to administer the estate. A resident factor in Stornoway is answerable to a small council of the residents. Commercial companies as owners appeared on the scene in Lewis after the lands were offered for sale when Leverhulme pulled out of his efforts to industrialise the Lewis folk. Considerable tracts of land were sold for as little as £500; some at 1p per acre. The salmon and trout fishings were, of course, a major attraction. Some small-acreage estates were bought in Harris and Lewis by speculators with island connections.

STORNOWAY

In contrast to the straggling and quite casual townships of the rural areas of the island, Stornoway has logic in its layout. The harbour and the grounds of Lews Castle have given the town a magnificent setting and a useful green belt surrounds it. The outlying villages, however, tend to be miracles of chaos, showing both architectural and planning anarchy. These only serve to add point to the more formal layout of Stornoway with its regular streets, some casual variation adding interest.

The town itself grew in recognisable stages. The first was centred on the small peninsula known as the Point Street area. This land finger protected the inner harbour of the Bayhead River and on it grew the nucleus of the town, beside old Stornoway Castle, once perched on a rocky islet and now existing as rubble under the steamer pier. Protection from storm was not really provided until the nineteenth century, when a quay was built with space for marketing and handling herring. About the seventeenth century, houses began to string themselves out along the shores on the side of the inner harbour (Bayhead Street and Cromwell Street) and on that side of the outer harbour called Newton Street. From the nineteenth century until about 1914, two-storey, flatted tenements, hotels and middle-class houses were built on a grid plan that followed on old field layouts and the associated ditches. Some of the present-day roads, such as James Street, follow these ditches, indicating perhaps the love of old-time planners for following existing lines and patterns. A plan of Stornoway drawn up by a John Wood in 1821 shows the town's development along definite grid lines with a few main streets, most of which were comparatively long and running south-north, seawards to landwards.

In 1918, when Lord Leverhulme made his bid to centralise the scattered, failing fishing industry of the island at Stornoway, he envisaged a further stage for the town. He began to build new houses, and had a grandiose proposal to reopen the diagonal arrangement indicated in John Wood's plan and centre it on some great new building. This fell through on his departure from Lewis; and since then, building here has become much the same as on the Scottish mainland.

In more recent years Stornoway has seen a kind of suburban development with, in particular, a new housing scheme of private dwellings in the same area as that proposed by John Wood. This area also contains the new primary school. A recent estimate of the cost of the building work, involving new houses and municipal facilities, amounted to almost £3 million. Municipal housing has been provided in smaller areas cleared of older houses. Of the 1600 houses in the Burgh, 50 per cent belong to the Burgh Council or the County Council, the balance being private.

HISTORY

FOR all that Harris and Lewis are remote and relatively inaccessible, their history has not been particularly insular. Out of all proportion to its size, the island has made a significant contribution to each developing phase of Scottish, British and Commonwealth history. Even European and American history have Hebridean touches. In a local context, each district in the island has a parti-coloured backcloth of history, of tradition, and of story against which life and events were enacted by each succeeding generation.

Before the era of charters, Harris was a political part of Lewis. The name is derived from 'heradh', meaning a district (equivalent to the modern parish). The word 'Lewis' has been tackled by etymologists who have extracted such meanings as 'light', 'Liot's dwelling', 'wharf' and the romantic 'songhouse'. But nearer the mark is 'a place abounding in pools', which it is. In its earliest form 'Lewis' appears in an Irish MS, the original of which is ascribed to a contemporary of the Irish king Brian Boroimhe (Brian Boru of the pipes fame).

The MS describes the Battle of Clontarf in 1014, at which Norsemen from Lewis fought against the Irish. It has been suggested that even before this time there was another name for Lewis. Pliny, Ptolemy and Solinus all place on their maps a variation of 'Hebrides': Hebudes, Ebudae. According to a Gaulish glossary, 'ebudae' means *terrains incultes*; and 'ebeid' is a British word meaning cornless. Solinus, writing in the third century BC, states that the inhabitants of the Hebrides did not know the use of corn, and lived entirely on fish and milk.

PREHISTORIC REMAINS

Where does history begin? That there was a pre-history is evidenced mainly by the multilithic and monolithic erections to be found in various parts of the island. The abundance and character of these prehistoric remains indicates that before the Christian era began the island supported a considerable population. Generally speaking, the remains left by unrecorded history indicate three phases of cultural and economic development: the Stone Age, the Bronze Age, and the Iron Age. The dates usually associated with these 'ages' are approximate where the island is concerned. Because of their remoteness and isolation, the inhabitants may well have reached, say, the Bronze Age state of civilisation at a much later date than did people living in more direct contact with civilising influences. It has been conjectured that, where Lewis is concerned, peat several feet thick may have covered much of the ground which, in another time, was cultivated and lived on; and that the peat blanket hides the remains of very old constructions. Chambered cairns, duns or forts (round towers) built in lochs, by the seashore and on promontories, galleried duns, earth houses, standing stones, stone circles and ecclesiastical ruins are all to be found.

The duns, or brochs, are believed to have had a defensive function, acting as lookout towers. Primitive dwellings would have been scattered nearby, with generally free-ranging livestock. If attack threatened, inhabitants and cattle together entered the tower, whose double walls held rough but welcome compartments for temporary living during the siege. Sometimes a dun was built on an islet in a freshwater loch, such as Dun Cromore in the Lochs district of Lewis; there is a similar example in Loch Bharabhat in Uig. A stone causeway connects each with the nearest point on the loch shore. Many of these causeways had a rocking-stone, a stepping stone so placed that the weight of a foot on it rocked it enough to warn the inmates of the dun that someone was approaching.

The most famous of the round towers is at Carloway, perched on the crest of a rocky slope on the west coast of Lewis near the crofting township of that name and overlooking much of Loch Roag. Its average external diameter is 47 ft, the walls varying in thickness from 10 to 12 ft. Though in a ruinous state, one side of its wall is still some 30 ft high. Dun Carloway is, after the broch on the Shetland isle of Mousa, the finest example of its kind in the country. About eight miles from Carloway, at Bragar, is Dun

Loch an Duna, now just a ruin. However, when Martin Martin saw it in 1695 (he seems to have ignored Dun Carloway), he described it as 'of a round form, made taperwise towards the top, and is three stories high: the wall is double, and hath several doors and stairs, so that one may go round within the wall.'

Most people have heard of the Callernish stones, and rightly so. For of all the world's megalithic monuments, only Callernish in Lewis is known to be arranged in the form of the Christian

The ruined broch or dun at Dun Carloway, on the west of Lewis. It was inhabited until the early eighteenth century, and ranks with the broch at Mousa, Shetlands, as a fine example of this type of structure. The purpose of these buildings is still debated

cross: a stone circle and four avenues of stones leading from it. It is reckoned that this stone circle was a great religious centre on a par with Stonehenge, Avebury and Carnac. There are a number of standing stones elsewhere in the island, both in Harris and Lewis; these stand singly or in small groups. Within four miles of Callernish are no less than seven smaller stone circles, and of these, including Callernish, three surround burial cairns. The Callernish circle is placed on a small rocky promontory of Loch Roag, easy to reach from both north and south parts of the island, with good anchorage in the Loch. The circle enclosing the cairn consists of thirteen stones and has a diameter of some 37 ft. The avenue, which approaches from the north, contains nineteen stones. It is 27 ft wide and 270 ft long; it forms the long limb of the cross plan of the design. Southward was another shorter avenue of twelve stones; and eastwards and westwards two lines of four stones each, thus completing the cross design. The stones range in height from $3\frac{1}{2}$ to $15\frac{1}{2}$ ft. Each is packed in at its base with small stones to keep it firmly in position. There are signs that Callernish, like Stonehenge, was built in stages. The material, unlike that used for Stonehenge, was from local sources (often Lewisian gneiss).

In the Sound of Harris, on the small island of Berneray, there are two stone circles of some interest. Scattered through Harris and Lewis there are also many solitary stones to be seen : at Borvemore, in Harris, which appears to have been one of a circle, and at Nisabost, also in Harris, where stands Clach MhicLeoid (MacLeod's Stone). Another standing stone is on the edge of the rocks by the shore, just below the church, on Boreray, one of the now-uninhabited islands in the Harris Sound. In Lewis, the menhir which figures most in story and legend is the Clach an Truiseil, on the gentle slope of a hillside near to Balantrusal, on the west coast. Nineteen feet of this stone are above ground. It is about 6 ft in width; nearly 4 ft at its maximum thickness. The tradition in Lewis is that the stone was erected to commemorate a victory by the Morisons of Ness over their long-standing enemies the MacAulays of Uig; of course the stone is older than any of the Lewis clans.

For a full inventory of the ancient and historical monuments, one is referred to the 1928 Report of the Royal Commission which was set up to record such constructions in the Outer Hebrides. Apart from those items of pre-Christian years, there are a number of other structures with an ecclesiological reference : Teampull Eoin, at Bragar; Teampull Pheadair, at Shader; Teampull Bhrighid, at Mid-Borve; Teampull nan Cro Naomh, at Galson; Teampull Ronaidh, at Eoropie, and others. These latter, together with the Tigh nan Cailleachan Dubh (house of the black old women), indicate a reasonable degree of saturation by some form of religious recognition; the names suggest a period about halfway

(*above*) The TSMV *Loch Seaforth*, built in 1947, on the Stornoway–Mallaig run until 1972

(*below*) The SS *Claymore* (1881–1931). The first ship built for the fleet of David
MacBrayne Ltd

(*above*) Driftnet fishing boats in Stornoway harbour. The new boats to form the basis for the island fleet of the future will be seine-net and dual-purpose

(*below*) The Lewis village of Gravir, showing small fishing boats in Loch Odhairn, 1932

to AD 1000. The base of the missionary work was most probably Iona. The old Celtic Church, with its monastic basis, sent out many who sought the hardship and solitude of life in the islands of the Hebrides as a means of example to the inhabitants. Today, the ancient cell sites, churches, burial-places, are in ruins, no more than a heap of grass-covered stones meriting scarcely a glance. Even on the outlier islands, such as the Shiants in the Minch and the Flannans in the Atlantic, are found these relics of ancient sites where the religious element was strong, overriding enough to be carried to the present day in traditional form.

From time to time archaeological finds are made in various parts of the island. Perhaps the most famous was the discovery of the Uig Chessmen, to be seen today in the Museum of Antiquities in Edinburgh and in the Ivory Room of the British Museum. In the spring of 1831 an exceptionally high tide, with a gale wind, undermined and carried away a considerable portion of a sand-bank at Ardroil, in Uig. A small stone building, like an oven, was exposed at some depth below the surrounding ground level. A crofter who happened to be working nearby saw this and, excited by curiosity, broke into the structure. On seeing what he thought to be an assembly of elves and gnomes, he fled home in great distress. His wife, of a bolder nature, went to see for herself and recovered ninety-two pieces of ivory figures: fourteen draughts-men, eight kings, eight queens, thirteen bishops, fifteen knights, and twelve footmen or pawns. These chess pieces, carved out of walrus ivory, date from about 1140 to 1160; they are of Norse origin, though probably carved by monastics who knew in detail the dress of the dignitaries which make up the set.

Some details of how the people of the Western Isles lived 3,800 years ago were revealed in an archaeological excavation in North-ton in 1966. This site showed evidence of more or less continuous habitation from the late Stone Age onwards; as each succeeding layer of sand was taken away (it was excavated to a depth of some 14 ft), centuries-old stages of habitation were revealed. The higher levels of the site belong to the Iron Age; the earlier levels date back to the late Neolithic/early Bronze Age (about 1800 BC). Such sites as this are extremely rare in Europe, and Northton is the only one of its date in Scotland. Many fragments of the pottery known

Artist's impression of some of the twelfth-century walrus-ivory chess pieces found at Uig in 1831

as beaker ware, from its distinctive shape, were recovered. The diet of these early Harris folk appears to have been largely shell-fish, particularly limpets. The house of the latest period is ruined; three courses of walling were revealed.

Placenames have often been a mirror of history. The biggest event in Harris and Lewis's history was the Norse invasion, commemorated in the names of many townships that still exist: Ness (nes, headland), Arnish (Ari's ness), Erisort (Eri's firth), Carloway (Karli's bay). But the Gaelic is there too : Loch Shell (Sealg, chase or hunt, thus endorsing Dean Monro's statement that this loch bordered a deer-forest), and similar topographical features. While the Norse names are to be found on the island coasts (the bosts and stads), the Gaelic names are largely found in the interior (eg, Airidhs—sheilings).

FIRE AND SWORD

Recorded history begins with the Icelandic sagas. In 1098 Magnus Bareleg plundered Lewis and devastated the island with both fire and sword. A skald named Bjorr Cripplehand, who accompanied Magnus on the expedition, reported that 'Fire played in the fig-trees of Liodhus; it mounted up to heaven. Far and wide the people were driven to flight. The fire gushed out of the houses.' The *Irish Annals* tell us that Skye was pillaged by the Norse in 794, and no doubt Lewis did not escape their attentions, then or earlier. Towards the end of the ninth century a stream of Norse folk left their homes to start the work of colonisation. Iceland, the Faroes, the Orkneys, the Shetlands and the Hebrides soon became thriving communities in which the earlier native population were as thralls, serving ruthless masters.

By about AD 1000, the island, with others as far south as Man, was in the sure and steady grip of men of Scandinavian or semi-Scandinavian origin, who were destined to become premier clans such as Clan Donald. It was not until the Battle of Largs in 1263 that this grip was loosened. In 1266 the Western Isles were ceded by Norway to Scotland, following which event the Gaelic people and their former Norse masters were soon to be merged in the marriage bed. As for the common language, it was the Celtic elements which took over after, one supposes, some generations of suppression. The result in any case was a highly individual people, strong in character, and resilient enough to take the rough times with the smooth.

In the thirteenth century, Harris was in the possession of the MacLeods of Harris, and Lewis belonged to three powerful clans : the Morisons in Ness, the MacAulays in Uig, and the MacLeods of Lewis in the remainder of the island. Other smaller clans were the MacIvers, the MacRaes, and the Nicolsons. The Harris Mac-Leods were allied by kinship to the Lewis MacLeods, though the relationship was to become quite distant—and their destiny more fortunate. History from this time is one of disputes, internecine warfare, murders, and similar crises deemed to be of the highest importance by the clans, both inside the island and between the islanders and strangers. An enormous amount of blood was spilled in the following two centuries as clan rivalry, with its claims and counter-claims for territorial and other rights, was predominant. Generally, what could not be taken by intermarriage was snatched by fiercer means.

Though these times generated a tradition of extraordinary richness, one must wonder what would have been the result had more attention been spared for the development of the island. Progress was retarded. The lawlessness was not worse than that endemic on much of the Scottish and English mainland or in Europe, but the island was of course more cut off from the gradual infiltration of civilising agencies and influences; at some times in its history it was found to be more than a century behind even the rest of Scotland.

MOVEMENTS TOWARD CIVILISATION

And what was the Scots Government in Edinburgh doing about the Western Isles? In the Middle Ages, the answer is very little. It had enough troubles of its own without endeavouring to police the clan warfare in that remote part of the kingdom; in any case the islands of the west were difficult to get to and probably best left alone. This attitude did not hold indefinitely. Once the semblance of peaceful conditions was established throughout the Scottish mainland, attention was duly focused further afield. In 1506 Stornoway Castle was beseiged and captured by the Earl of Huntly—the first time cannon and gunpowder were used in the Western Isles, and the first of a number of punitive expeditions arranged to bring the unruly clans to heel.

One of the leaders of disorder at this time was Roderic Mac-Leod of Lewis, and it was to parley with him that no less a person than James V decided to visit the island. In 1540 James, with devastating swiftness, determined to quell these fighting chiefs once and for all, arrived to examine conditions on the spot. Titles to land were closely looked at and the equivalent of our 'small print' read carefully. All the chiefs who owned anything in the islands were forced to accompany the King on his tour of inspection. No doubt this close contact resulted in James becoming as fluent in the Gaelic language as his father had been in his time.

For Gaelic was still spoken in most parts of Scotland, and it was the language which the chiefs themselves understood to the last fine shade. James's visit was followed by a period of unusual calm, ensured by the detention of hostages; in Lewis, the brew of trouble had been turned down to a simmer.

After the death of the chief of the Lewis MacLeods, Roderic, however, rival dynastic claims turned up the heat again. Newcomers appeared on the scene : the MacKenzies of Kintail. Carefully they manipulated the events of history, indeed twisted them, until with the Crown on their side they had established beyond doubt that they were legally entitled to Lewis. In many ways, Lewis was fortunate in its new proprietor, Kenneth MacKenzie, Lord Kintail. Both he and his successor, Colin, the first Earl of Seaforth, were enlightened men, of different calibre from those they had displaced. They were in close contact with the immediate outside world, the emerging Scotland; and they were familiar with the amenities which that world offered. They were also aware of the needs of a community little removed from the early phases of cultural progress. In particular Seaforth, a man of ability and foresight, recognised, as did others before him, that the prosperity of the island had to be based on fish. He was also aware of the value of strong connections with Church and education. The Lewis historian, W. C. MacKenzie, writes :

At the end of the seventeenth century, the picture we have of Lewis is that of a people pursuing their avocations in peace, but not in plenty. The Seaforths had been extravagant, and the people had to pay for their extravagances; they were politicians, and the people had to pay for their politics. Yet, it is clear that, besides establishing orderly Government in the island, they had done a good deal to rescue the people from the slough of ignorance and incivility in which they found themselves immersed. But in the sphere of economics their policy apparently was of little service to the community.

Under the Seaforths, Lewis became involved in external affairs. During the times of the Covenanting troubles, it sent a contingent to the Battle of Auldearn, where the Covenanters were defeated by Montrose. At the Battle of Worcester, one of the two leaders of the thousand MacLeods taking part in that 'stiff fight' was

Norman MacLeod, of Bernera, Harris. The result of the Seaforth family becoming involved in royalist activities was that Lewis was occupied by a Cromwellian garrison. Their station was close by old Stornoway Castle, now a heap of rubble under Stornoway's modern quays; and later a fort was built from the stones of the Castle, broken down by the English. The affair of the 'Fifteen', 1715, again brought Lewis into prominence. And a considerable part of the force raised for the Earl of Mar was recruited there. Four years later, plans for yet another Rising were hatched out at Seaforth Lodge, near where Lews Castle now stands. Only indirectly was Lewis involved in the last rising, the 'Forty-five'. Prince Charles Edward, a fugitive, reached Stornoway in search of a ship which would get him away from the cold western islands to the warmth of France. He met an indifferent welcome. The townspeople, weary of past punishment, gave him no help; nor, despite the large reward on the Prince's head, did they do him harm or betray him. Today, at Arnish Point, at the mouth of Stornoway Bay, a cairn commemorates the visit of that ill-fated man, the falling star in the Stuart firmament.

THE FIFE ADVENTURERS

One of the main episodes in Lewis history in the early years of the island's emergence as an area worthy of commercial exploitation was the expedition of the Fife Adventurers. Towards the end of the sixteenth century, the name of Lewis was being mentioned in the same breath as 'profit'. At that time, Lewis was in a state of anarchy. The deeds, misdeeds, and defiance of both law and order by Roderick MacLeod, chief, were enough to inspire any central authority with a zeal to convert the island and bring it to heel. And if, by happy chance, it were to become profitable to the converters, they would be well rewarded. The 'civilisation' of a territory has often been forcible, bringing the inhabitants suddenly and painfully into a new air of living, in which the things that it seemed reasonable to do yesterday are done today on pain of death. In Scotland at that time, recognition of the law and the Church were the prime factors of civilisation, such as it was, the marks of superiority. Lewis, on the other hand, had a barbarous air about it; the Lewismen, said an official indictment, had 'given themselves over to all kynd of barbaritie and inhumanitie', and they were 'voyd of ony knawledge of God or His religion'. Thus the people of Lewis had something coming to them.

For some time King James VI of Scotland (James I of England) had been concerned with the problem of bringing the MacLeods of Lewis into an awareness of his authority. His 'maill' and 'gressum', the duties owed to him by the MacLeods, were long overdue; there was nothing for it but to go and collect. The fact that Lewis had been described to him as 'inrychit with ane incredibill fertilitie of cornis and store of fischeingis and utheris necessaris, surpassing far the plenty of any pairt of the inland' probably inspired his scheme to gather it all within the hem of his cloak. Whether he was aware of the true level of the island's produce is not known; though the sea was rich indeed. In any event, the scheme was nothing if not predatory. The 'civilisation' motive was a veneer to cover up any action deemed necessary to secure the island for the Crown. A contract was drawn up between the King and the Adventurers. These men, drawn largely from Fife, were also inspired by the supposed El Dorado lying just beyond the mountains of the Highlands and the waters of the Minch. An adventure it was thought, for Lewis was as remote to the Fifers as the Americas were to the Spaniards; and an adventure it proved to be. The Adventurers landed in November 1598. Lewis showed them little signs of welcome. Cold, high winds, rain, bleak cliffs, and a Gaelic-speaking people whom they could not understand met them; and to compensate for the chill of the season, MacLeod of Lewis gave them a warm-up fight. But the mercenaries which the Adventurers brought with them proved the better men for a time.

Resistance overcome, the incomers established themselves as best they could. They built a 'prettie toun' in the part of Stornoway known as South Beach, facing Stornoway Bay. That small curve of land is still there today, probably as it was almost 400 years ago. Food ran short. The Adventurers had thought that this land of milk and plenty would supply them with sufficient provisions on arrival; so they had brought only emergency stores. Starvation forced them to obtain what they could locally, as best

they could. Winter winds and the damp climate brought many
to an early deathbed; dysentery ran rife. A message was sent south
to obtain relief, but the messenger was captured at sea by one of
the MacLeods. Again a message was sent. And hardly had this
errand of mercy sailed out of sight than the MacLeods descended
on the 'toun' with 'two hundred barbarous, bludie, and wiket
Hielandmen' to attack the Adventurers and kill twenty-two of
them, burn some property and make off with livestock. In fact,
the methods which the Adventurers had hoped to used on the
islanders to 'civilise' them were now being turned on themselves,
to prevent the resented conversion. They left Lewis in a black
cloud of despair. In 1605 they made another attempt. Again they
were met by the MacLeods under the leadership of Neil Mac-
Leod, who prevented all endeavours to establish a Fife colony on
the island. Four years later a last bid was made to bring the
island and its resources under their control. And again they
failed.

In 1610, after the collapse of the third colonisation attempt by
the Adventurers, they sold their charter rights to Kenneth Mac-
Kenzie of Kintail who, from the very beginning of the scheme,
had veered hot and cold to the Crown, the Adventurers, and the
Lewismen. His reward for his craft was Lewis—though it took
him a further two years to reduce the MacLeods to accepting
him as the new owner of the island.

UNDER THE COMMONWEALTH

Cromwell and England : the two names are so allied that it seems
to strain fiction to link Cromwell and Lewis, more particularly
Stornoway. Yet the main shopping street in the town has been,
from about the 1820s, 'Cromwell Street'; when, or why, or who,
changed its former title of 'Dempster Street' are matters lost forever. Cromwell himself was never in Lewis, but he did once take
an interest in it.

The island took his attention, firstly, because its owner, a youth
of sixteen who was later Earl of Seaforth, was 'playing rex' there.
When Scotland was subjugated by the English Commonwealth,
and the administration was placed in the hands of General Monk,

a group of Highland Royalists refused to submit. Among them was the youthful Seaforth. At the time he was rich; he belonged to a powerful and influential family; and he could call up many hundreds of claymores. He could hardly be ignored.

The second factor which disturbed Cromwell was the island's position. When the war between the Commonwealth and Holland broke out, it was seen that co-operation between Highland malcontents and the Dutch could prove to be a source of great danger for England; Stornoway had the best harbour on the west coast of Scotland and, as Cromwell wrote, the Dutch 'had an eye on it'. Events were accelerated by an incident in Stornoway harbour in May 1653, when Seaforth caused some offence to the captain of a privateer, the *Fortune*. When Seaforth discovered the vessel to be in the employ of the Commonwealth, he arrested the boat's crew and offered them terms of surrender. Captain Brassie replied with a couple of broadsides on the town and sailed away to complain to Colonel Lilburn, who had succeeded Monk as commander-in-chief in Scotland. An example had to be made; defiance of the Commonwealth had to be put down. 'I doubt nott,' he reported to Cromwell, 'but what wee may be able to doe uppon that island, will soe startle the whole Highlands and Islands that wee shall nott bee much troubled with them in such like cases hereafter. Undoubtedly to make the Lord Seaforth and his island (called the Lewes) exemplary will bee a very great advantage to the peace of this nation.'

Under the command of Colonel Cobbet, a military force, with warships and provision ships, was sent from Leith to take possession of Lewis. Some resistance was put down with a bit of trouble. A report in a contemporary London newspaper indicates that an attack by the Lewismen (who had fled to the hills, and who were armed with bows and arrows) was so fierce that the English were 'constrained to make face about'. The resistance was overcome, however, and Cobbet placed Lewis in the charge of a Major Crispe and a garrison of four companies. This garrison settled down to the task of making Lewis secure against possible attacks by the Dutch. A fort was built in Stornoway, and some armouring was undertaken at the small Goat Island in Stornoway Bay. A ground-plan of the 'Cromwellian' fortifications is in Worcester College, Oxford University, with an estimated date of 1653, the year in which the English garrison was placed in Lewis. Nothing now remains of that fort built by Crispe's soldiers, though the whole area on the small point of land, present-day Point Street, is redolent of historical atmosphere, despite new buildings.

RELIGIOUS HISTORY

Ecclesiology is a horse of many different colours in the island. Tradition goes right back to the early stirrings of Christianity in Scotland. Indeed, one of the most important religious sites on the island is St Columba's at Eye, near Aignish, some seven miles from Stornoway. Though the name might suggest it, there is no proof that the Gaelic abbot visited Lewis. But it is more than likely that a follower of his did so in his name. Part of the church at Eye is Norman, which gives an approximate date of origin, though it is necessary to take some account of the long interval between a development phase in one country and its adoption in another country quite insulated from change, as were the Outer Isles in medieval times. According to tradition, the church was built on the site of a cell occupied by the Celtic saint Catan, who is believed to have lived in the sixth or seventh century. Possibly this is the same Catan to whom a shrine is dedicated at Mealasta, in Uig, close by which the remains of a nunnery have been found, called by a Gaelic name meaning 'the house of the old black women'.

St Columba's is mentioned in records from 1506, when it is described as a 'rectory'. At present, though in a ruined state, it still shows its former strength of character, both as a building, a place of sanctuary, and a place of worship. It has also been called the Valhalla of Lewis, for tradition says that some nineteen Chiefs of Siol Torquil, the MacLeods of Lewis, are buried in its grounds. William, the fifth Earl of Seaforth, also found there an uneasy bed beside the enemies of his ancestors, who wrested Lewis from the MacLeods.

Another significant church is St Olaf's, or St Molua's at Eoropie, at the Butt of Lewis. Recorded evidence first indicates the existence of the church in 1630, where it occurs in a report by Captain Dymes. The saint laboured mainly in the Hebrides; he died in the north of Scotland and was buried at Rosemarkie, on the Scottish mainland. Tradition ascribes the building of the church to the tenth century by King Olaf of Norway; though a a more realistic date for its foundation is the fourteenth century. That it occupies, as so many other small churches do, the site of a former cell is quite acceptable. The church, so Dymes tells us, had a 'sanctum sanctorum', so holy in fact that no women were ever allowed to enter it.

In Harris, the outstanding religious building is St Clement's, at Rodel, described in Chapter 8. There are, sprinkled like a measured largesse, small ruins of chapels, cells, oratories and wells; but only tradition has clothed these tumbled stones with the airs of the once-living. A map of the island will show up these sites, which are well worth a visit if only to spend a short time in reflection under the island sky beside ancient stones.

Other old ruins are to be found on the island of Calum Cille (Columba) in Loch Erisort. It is on record that the monks who came from Iona to convert the islanders from pagan forms of religion to Christianity landed on the island about the middle of the sixth century. They founded a church with its burial ground, which they dedicated to their master, hence the Gaelic names: Eaglais, Cladh, agus Eilean Chalum Chille. Tradition also mentions a mill, Muileann-na-manach, but there is not one stone left on another to indicate its exact site. The old burial ground served the parish of Lochs for many generations until about a century ago. The people of the island were in medieval and post-medieval times profoundly religious; this reverence was more often than not carried over into the half-world of superstition.

Though the tangible remains of religion's progress are to be seen, the recorded history of religious progress, its phases and developments, is scant. One can only assume that it was the Columban Church which first introduced the new Christianity to the Lewis folk. The earlier religion was the stock on to which the new was grafted. The result was an amalgam which was nothing if not strange to those many visitors who came to comment on the island scene; for it was neither Christian nor heathen. Yet, again, a strong thread of veneration ran through the product which firmly held the folk. The Reformed Church of Scotland did little in the later centuries in Lewis. The Fife Adventurers brought a clergyman with them, a Robert Durie, minister of Anstruther, but it can be taken that his ministrations were for the benefit of the Fifers. The aborigines were left to their own brand of faith, to find grace as and where they could.

The interregnum between the abolition of Romanism and the effective establishment of the Reformed Church in the islands was marked by a decline in the 'Christian-ness' of the people. Former teachings were forgotten, and it is no coincidence that in this interim period social anarchy was rife. The credit for restoring Christian principles to Lewis rests with a Farquhar MacRae, vicar of Gairloch, a young man of about thirty years of age whom Lord Kintail brought to Lewis in 1610. On his arrival he found it necessary to baptise all under forty years of age, and practically to reintroduce the institution of marriage. The first Earl of Seaforth was a religious man; he built St Lennan's church in Stornoway, now non-existent, on North Beach. In 1626 there were two ministers in Lewis (Barvas and Eye), and gradually the influence of religion was restored.

ISLAND REGIMENTS

It is a natural enough step from wielding a sword in the protection of one's home island to bearing arms for King and Country. After the 'natives had been pacified' over a period of a century or so, the national call to arms came north across the Hebrid seas. The warlike character of the clans in the north of Scotland had not escaped the notice of those charged with keeping England and the later Britain busy with overseas interests which required some military backing to maintain and improve. Lewis, in particular, despite its small size, has over the past couple of centuries contributed much of great importance both in regiments and fighting men; its military history is a subject that has escaped many past writers on the island.

There is possibly no British regiment more closely associated with historic deeds of heroism than the Seaforths, the Seaforth Highlanders. At the turn of the eighteenth and nineteenth centuries, many villages in the north of Scotland suffered from the attentions of ship-borne press-gangs, who swooped down on unsuspecting communities and whisked away the best of the males they could find. Lewis did not escape this enforced service. Local traditions have much to say about compulsion, though not by press-gang. Young men were pressed into service through personal influence, by bribe or by blackmail. However, in the case of the Seaforth Highlanders, the raising of recruits was by appeal to the men of the clan and the clan adherents.

The first battalion of Seaforths was raised in December 1777 by Kenneth, the sixth Earl of Seaforth. By far the greater number of soldiers were from the MacKenzie estates on the mainland : from Applecross, Kintail, and Lochalsh. Few Lewismen served among the soldiers of Coinneach Og, as the Earl was called. The real beginning of the Seaforth Regiment was in March 1793, when a Letter of Service was granted to Lord Seaforth. The chief himself personally toured his estates for recruits, to offer the King's Shilling. His visit to Lewis was at first regarded with some suspicion; he even met some active opposition in Uig, which was overcome by his explanation of the country's need to counteract the widespread effects of the high tide of the social revolution begun in France. In 1804, another battalion was raised; some 200 Lewismen volunteered, a fact recounted in tradition with great pride. The history of the regiment in those early formative years is detailed with battles in many parts of the world: Nimogen in Holland, Quiberon Bay in Brittany, Cape Town, India (Assaye is remembered in a Stornoway street name), Java, Messina, and so on.

In Egypt, many a Lewis lad found himself face to face with the Turks, and subsequently in a slave market in Cairo. One of the old soldiers of Uig has left traditions of his seven years' experience as a prisoner of the Turks. Some youths who had volunteered for service early in life were so ignorant of their island's geography that they found themselves in Stornoway on their return looking around for a guide to show them the way across the moors to their long-left homes. The hot, white sun of Egypt brought loss of sight to many soldiers, who returned to a Lewis which they could never see again. Some who were blinded at

Rosetta were granted a pension of about £30 per annum, with an allowance of £12 per annum for a guide to lead them about.

On 21 December 1859, 'a public meeting of the Inhabitants of Stornoway was held in the Mason Hall to consider the propriety of organising an Artillery Volunteer Corps for the defence of this Island'. About a month later, Sir James Matheson, Baronet of Achany, and Member of Parliament for the Lews, was asked to tender to Her Majesty the services of eighty-one gentlemen who wished to form the corps. The unit eventually formed was the 1st Company in the County of Ross and held the 44th place in the Artillery Volunteer Force of Great Britain. After many ups and downs in its history, this corps exists today as the Ross Battery.

For more than half a century the activities of the corps were peaceful. The only highlight was its participation in the famous Wet Review at Edinburgh, on the occasion of Queen Victoria's Jubilee. Matching the rain which lashed down in sheets from the sky, a sewer burst open in the centre of the parade ground. Company after company divided ranks as they approached the disagreeable fountain in their path. But Lt John N. Anderson, later Provost of Stornoway, gave the order 'Right into it!' Amid a great roaring of cheers from the watching crowds, the Stornoway Volunteers marched straight on in perfect order. It was perhaps prophetic of the sterner tests to come.

The unit was one of the Royal Garrison Artillery in 1908 when it was reformed as the Ross Mountain Battery of the 4th Highland (Mountain) Brigade. Later, as a regular division, the battery was·the first field artillery to be landed at Cape Helles, in the Gallipoli campaign. At Suvla Bay, it lost 50 per cent of its strength in two days. At Ismailia it mustered again to fight against the Turks in the Canal area, but it was not allowed to remain to assist in driving back the enemy. Instead, it was moved to Salonika to help the mountain batteries, now much depleted by malaria. The final move was to Bulgaria, where the Lewismen were the first gunners, if not the first British troops, to enter that country.

Before, during, and for a time after, the first world war, the Ross Battery had close ties with the Nicolson Institute. To quote from a past Rector of the school:

For a number of years it had been the practice for a considerable proportion of the older schoolboys during their attendance at the Secondary School to put in their training with the local body of Territorials—the Ross Mountain Battery. At the School Prizegiving of 1914, these boys attended in their uniform to be ready to go off the same evening by steamer en route for the annual training camp. Before the School re-opened, the Territorial Force was mobilised, and for some of these lads there intervened four long years of toil, of fighting, and of sickness overseas, before they ever saw their homes again.

Later (1938), the unit became the 203rd (Ross) Battery of the 51st (West Highland) Anti-tank Regiment. It was whilst fighting as an anti-tank battery that, with other units of the 51st Division, the men were taken prisoner at St Valery in 1940. Today, after more changes, the battery is the oldest in 540 LAA Regt RA, TA (the Lovat Scouts). In 1960 the Ross Battery received the Freedom of the Burgh of Stornoway in recognition of a century of voluntary service to the community and the nation.

LAND USE AND CROFTING

The history of land use and the crofting system in the Highlands and Islands (see Chapter 5) is full of difficulties. In the older days of the clan system, before the rot set in, though the clan members belonged to the chief, they also belonged to the land and the land to them. In such a climate, the agricultural system, for it was such then, was in a reasonably healthy state; the land was worked to the full. Good land was available for the support of the clan, and as often as not in good years there was ample produce, crops, and livestock, to send south to well-paying markets. That fertile lands abounded is indicated by the reports of visitors in various centuries. But times changed. The increase in population after the breakdown of the clan system by statutory legislation, and the policy of population placement carried out with a rigorous enthusiasm, planted seeds of discontent—in particular a hunger for land. The land was in any case becoming ever more inadequate to support those already on it.

The story of the agrarian troubles in the Highlands area is well

51

documented; and Harris and Lewis played out their part in the agitation for more land. Briefly, when the clan system was broken down, the clansman found himself freed of the obligation of service to the chief. The chief, on his side, found himself thrown to the economic dogs. Payments in kind were no currency; a house in London or in Edinburgh had to be paid for in cash, and a London hairdresser would hardly accept half a dozen eggs for his services. The effect of the Heritable Jurisdictions Act was like a butcher's chopper. With a stroke a social organisation was given notice to change overnight, with no period of transition allowed. The chiefs looked to the land for their money. In the old system, their prosperity had been largely measured in fighting men. Now the pressures of economics demanded increased rents from those who were being called tenants. Increased rents can, however, be paid only when the land's productivity rises. The agricultural changes percolating through the Lowlands of Scotland had not even begun to penetrate to the Highlands area. Many tenants found that, unable to pay the increased rent demands, they were ejected from the lands which, incidentally, they had held by traditional understanding—written deeds were rare. Emigration started, and the vacant lands went to sheep-farmers, well able to pay good money for the grazings.

Some chiefs did give their tenants time to change to new methods of land use, and were careful not to make a breach between agriculture and grazing. Their tenants in turn improved the land, changing in particular from the old run-rig system, whereby a man working a piece of ground one year had the same piece the following year only if the dice were thrown his way. But the class of farmers' tenants called crofters (who had no security of tenure) or cottars (a squatter type with no legal recognition) found themselves on the verge of starvation. The few acres of ground they had, or to which they had been removed, were quite unsuitable for intensive cultivation to produce even the basic necessities of life.

The picture of land use was that of a great black pot boiling furiously with a brew of which the final taste was quite uncertain. When the boiling was controlled, the land began to be parcelled out, a share to each family. This led to a rigid, almost monolithic,

(*above*) At Rishgarry Quay, Isle of Berneray, in the Sound of Harris, c 1900, showing the typical construction of the 'black house'

(*below*) The Claddach, Isle of Killegray, in the Sound of Harris, April 1897. The horse and cart was the most convenient means of transport. A spinning wheel is seen in action

The hills of North Harris. On the far side of the loch (West Loch Tarbert) can be seen the remains of the whaling station

agrarian order. Crofting townships were created which contained holdings of a uniform size, often fit to provide only a bare subsistence living. This is still so today. There were and are no means of achieving ambition through some kind of agricultural promotion, no ladder to climb to prove one's ability to win the land over to one's side to increase its yield. And as each family increased, the progeny demanded land. The family acres were divided, subdivided and fragmented to a vicious mathematical system: more people, less land.

In the nineteenth century, many estates were sold. The newcomers, with no kinship ties with the small tenantry, saw that the only way to make their estates economic was to establish large farms, which meant the eviction, by force if necessary, of the small tenants. This is what happened. For those who did not emigrate, it was a life of huddling around a weak fire, whose flame itself could hardly stand, and thinking of the prospect of starvation and the 'old days'. Thoughts nourished on these old days became the root of action; and a fierce agitation for land reform started. The Minutes of Evidence of the Napier Commission (1882-4), of the Deer Forest Commission (1894-6) and the several official reports on the conditions of the crofters and cottars, give ample evidence of bitterness and despair as the result of poverty and lack of opportunity. About 1870, unrest in the congested areas of crofting townships became a political issue. The flames of ideals were burning high and bright. Ideals were transformed into action: take the land!

By 1880, the ripples from the stone flung into the agrarian pond were reaching the general public. Sides were taken: one stood either on the economic touchline, or on that dangerous thin red line of sentiment based on high feelings and a deep sense of wrongs being perpetrated on fellow humans. The landowners naturally insisted on the right to move into an era of land use in which management was not hampered by affairs of sentiment or philanthropy. Governed by the cold principles of business, they hardened themselves in the face of their attackers. And though they pointed to arrears in rent, and their inability to improve their land agriculturally while they had tenants not of their own choosing, they faced mounting antagonism.

55

The crofters were in a state of revolt against the accumulation of trends and events which now stood like a high dam against their progress to a higher level of acceptance in the social scene. They stood in open conflict with local and national authority. Unhappy scenes were enacted, many being in complete variance with the natural temperament of the Highlander. Lewis crofters were not far behind with their contribution to the agitation for land reform, though they had perhaps suffered less direct action from land-owners than had crofters in the Highlands and southern Islands. But their living conditions had deteriorated. And an inhumanly-efficient factor made for deep unrest.

Land agitation began in Lewis in 1881, and large numbers of Lewis crofters gave evidence before the Napier Commission. This Commission was the result of agitation for an enquiry into croft-ing conditions in the Highlands. Its setting up relieved a situation of acute tension, though it neither extinguished political agitation nor mitigated the disaffection felt in the more disturbed districts. Under Lord Napier's direction a mass of information was col-lected. The official findings of the Commission were almost identi-cal with political declarations in the country, but did not alto-gether coincide with the requirements of the crofters and their spokesmen. The resultant Crofters' Act of 1886 fixed the crofting system into that rigid trance in which agricultural innovation, opportunity for improvement, the social progress of crofting com-munities are largely lacking. It did give all crofters permanency of tenure, where they had none before, fair rents for the land they had and compensation for improvements. But the old demand for new smallholdings and settlements persisted with greater insistence and further pressure on high political circles.

In 1888, members of the new Crofters Commission visited Lewis and found that poverty was so general in the island that among 607 crofters for whom fair rents were fixed, there were scarcely a dozen who had not been recipients of 'destitution' meal or some other form of relief. The population was too much for the land to support it under the distribution system prevailing. The number of persons per family in 1871 was on average 5·358, as compared with 4·232 on the mainland of Ross and Cromarty, the county of which Lewis formed a part. Thirty years later, in

1901, the average was only 5·086, the county average being 3·983. The population was still to reach its peak in Lewis, some 30,000 in 1911. Emigration was at a fairly high rate, some 2,000 every decade, but this was no relief with births between 8,000 and 9,000 during the same period. In 1894 it was estimated that the number of cottars (or squatters) as distinct from crofters was in the region of 1,000. These people, mostly relatives of crofters, constituted a serious incubus on every crofting township.

Elsewhere in the Highlands, the enlargement of crofting holdings relieved the land-hunger situation. It was not possible for the same to be done in Lewis, and Harris possessed even less useful land to share out. Many applications were made by crofters either for an increase in their own holdings or an increase in the acreage of common grazings held by each township. Though some 500 acres were in fact handed over by the estate management for crofting purposes, there was a steady refusal to diminish the acreage of farms.

The Congested Districts Board was appointed in 1897, supervising public works to relieve the people of a certain amount of their ills. It carried on until 1912, when it passed into the newly-formed Board of Agriculture. The Congested Districts Board could have achieved much more than it did. It scraped away only a little of the vast problem. The next major landmark in the history of crofting legislation was the Small Landholders (Scotland) Act of 1911. It extended certain provisions introduced for the crofter in 1886, and further increased the class of tenants who benefited by bringing in the tenants of holdings rented at not more than £50 (£30 in Lewis) or not exceeding 50 acres (30 acres in Lewis). The 1911 Act also brought into existence the Scottish Land Court in place of the Crofters Commission. In Lewis, however, the hunger for more land went on unabated and reached a not insignificant peak during the later years of Lord Leverhulme's regime.

A new Crofters Commission was set up in 1955, following on the report of a Commission of Enquiry under the chairmanship of the then Principal T. M. Taylor of Aberdeen University. Fresh provision for the reorganisation, development and regulation of the crofting system in the seven crofting counties of Scotland was made in the Crofters (Scotland) Bill of 1961; this had a mixed reception. In general, today, small crofts predominate in most areas. Out of some 18,000 (the number is decreasing annually) about 15 per cent exceed 20 acres (see Chapter 5). But size has little to do with the type of land; whether arable or rough grazing. In fact, the proportion indicates that some 85 per cent of all crofts in Scotland, and this applies to Harris and Lewis, cannot be considered as full-time now or as potentially full-time.

EDUCATION

In general, the Highlands and Islands of Scotland owe their introduction to letters to the early Christian missionaries. One of the main provisions in the early monastic Church in Ireland and Scotland was for the cultivation of learning and the training of its members in sacred and profane literature. Associated as they were so closely with the common folk on the one hand and the aristocracy on the other, something of this learning and desire for learning rubbed off to advantage on to willing recipients. Literacy however, has had many ups and downs since the dawning of the Christian era in the Hebrides. Though it is impossible to ascertain to what extent the common folk participated in the knowledge imparted by the early Celtic monasteries, there are many references to a class of cleric called 'scolocs', whose learning was accessible to the poorer classes of the emergent Highland society. The 'scoloc' is still retained in Gaelic as 'sgalag', a farm servant, the poor searcher after knowledge who received education in the monasteries in return for services as labourer on the church lands, and who appears in monastic records as late as the fourteenth century.

As late as the sixteenth century, however, after the influence of the Church had diminished, the inhabitants were almost wholly illiterate. When the Fife Adventurers came to Lewis in 1598, they brought a schoolmaster with them; though it can be taken that his services were intended for the improvement of the incomers rather than the islesfolk. Old Roderic MacLeod, doughty chief of the MacLeods of Lewis at the time of the Fifers' arrival, was unable to sign his name. Two of his sons, on the other hand, were so literate as to have drawn up a bond, unaided and with a remarkable degree of legal precision.

It was not until Lewis belonged to the Seaforth family that anything in the nature of education generally came the way of the common folk of the island. John Morison, a native of Lewis, who wrote about 1680, says:

> Onlie for the tyme the countris is possessed and saglie governed by the Earle of Seaforth, by whose industrious care and benevolence the people, formerly inclined to rudeness and barbarity, are reduced to civilitie, much understanding and knowledge by the flourishing schooll planted and maintained by the said Earle all the tyme in the toun of Stornoway. And not onlie the people of the Lews, but also those of the nixt adjacent Isles. The gentlemens sons and daughters are bred in that schooll to the great good and comfort of that people; so that there are few families but at least the maister can read and write: I do remember in my own tyme that there was not three in all the countrie that knew A. b. by A Bible.

Martin Martin mentions this Stornoway school as teaching both Latin and English. During the eighteenth century a school for teaching both these subjects with writing and arithmetic was established.

Martin also indicates that it was never considered necessary or desirable to educate girls, whether they were common folk or daughters of the upper classes, unless they were daughters of chiefs and next in line to succeed their father, there being no male issue before them. Towards the close of the eighteenth century, efforts were made to educate the children of the island. Parochial schools had by that time been established; the Society in Scotland for Propagating Christian Knowledge and the Gaelic School Society supported several. Clergymen of the period, however, claimed that the advantages of education were not appreciated; as a consequence, the schools were not well attended.

The SSPCK had its origins in 1701, when a few private gentlemen met in Edinburgh and resolved to establish schools in the Highlands and Islands, and to appeal to the public for subscriptions for the purpose. They had a fitful beginning, but Queen Anne encouraged the scheme by royal proclamation and subscriptions flowed in. In 1709 the Queen granted Letters Patent under the Great Seal for erecting certain of the subscribers into a corporation. Thus did the SSPCK come into being, with an initial capital fund of £1,000. Its progress was rapid. In 1711, it supported twelve schools; in 1795, 323 schools. In addition to paying the teachers' salaries, the Society supplied the children with school books, established public libraries in various parishes, and defrayed the expenses of printing Gaelic Bibles and other books.

Harris here enters in an interesting sideline. In the records of the Presbytery of Mull, 1730, it is reported that 'Mr M'Aula . . . carried off the library to Harris, because he was not paid for his expenses in bringing them [the books of the Society] to Coll.' This MacAulay was the great-grandfather of the English man of letters, Lord MacAulay.

The Gaelic School Society was founded in 1811 and existed until 1892. It supported a large number of schools, as the desire for education had exceeded the capacity of the SSPCK. In 1796 there were two schools and a spinning school in the parish of Stornoway. The minister of Barvas, writing in that year, says that there had not been a parochial school in that parish for many years, but that there was a Society school at Ness, attended by about twenty pupils, instead of treble that number had all the children been made to attend. The minister of Uig stated that three spinning schools were established there by Lady Seaforth, but he does not refer to ordinary schools in his parish at that time. According to the minister of Lochs, a parochial school was built there in 1795, and a Society school some three years earlier.

By the middle of the nineteenth century matters had improved considerably, though there were still complaints that education was not appreciated. In fact, education tended to be discouraged for a very practical reason. Back in 1811 an observer in the island stated in his report that the great mass of the Lewis people would not send their children to school. 'When reproached on this head they answer "If we give them education, they will leave us."' Seventy-two years later (1883), the Napier Commission was told that 'Sir James (Matheson) supported and contributed to seventeen schools in the Island, many of which he built with teachers' houses prior to 1854. Monthly returns of attendance were sent to my office, and parents who did not keep their children at school were dealt with, but in many cases to no avail, as they often told me they did not want to give their children wings to leave them.'

In 1833 there were thirteen schools in the parish of Stornoway, according to the *New Statistical Account*, 1840-46, which records that there were 586 children between the ages of six and fifteen years, and 1,265 persons above the age of fifteen in the parish who could not read. Barvas had three schools in 1836; Uig had five in 1833. In Lochs, in 1833 a parish school had just been erected, and four schools were maintained by the Gaelic School Society; yet out of a parish population of 3,067, only 12 could write. After the Disruption of 1843, the Free Church established a large number of schools throughout the island. And soon after Sir James Matheson took over the island he built schools in those districts not catered for by other agencies.

In 1865, the Government began to prepare for the Education Act of 1872, and sent Sheriff-Substitute Nicolson to the island to investigate the state of education there. At the time of his visit there were forty-seven schools, supported by as many as nine different agencies, persons, or institutions. The number of pupils on the rolls was 3,332, with 2,647 in actual attendance. Nicolson computed that there were some 2,500 children on the island who did not normally attend school, and who should have done. A large number of schools were little more than thatched houses. Fifteen were good; fourteen tolerable; and eighteen bad or inadequate. In the third group he classes 'those that cannot by any standard of comfort or fitness above that of troglodyte, be considered suitable for having the work of education carried on in them, or any work indeed, to which the prevalence of smoke and moisture are infavourable.' Of the children who attended these schools, 79 per cent received tuition in the Scriptures; 85 per cent were taught to read; 39 per cent were taught writing; 32 per cent were taught arithmetic; and 16 per cent taught needlework.

The Education Act of 1872 put an end to the old parochial system, and virtually to other agencies which it found at work. The schools on the island were brought into line with the remainder of Scotland where, under the school boards, education became both free and compulsory.

In Lewis the school of real significance to the island was, and still it, the Nicolson Institute, founded by Alexander Morison Nicolson and opened in February 1873, supported by bequests from him and his brothers. Nicolson's grandfather was the founder of the Lewis fish-curing trade, and was also shipowner and farmer. Alexander was the fifth of six sons and was educated in Stornoway parish school and in Glasgow High School. He served an apprenticeship as an engineer with Thomson of Clydebank. Later he entered the service of the Chinese Government and established himself with a partner of a shipbuilding and foundry business in Shanghai. In 1865, in his thirty-third year, he was killed in a boiler explosion in one of his new ships going a trial run. His ideal of establishing a school in Stornoway was subscribed to by his brothers who were a widespread family: Yorkshire, Mississippi, Western Australia, Tighnabruaich (Scotland) and South Africa.

The first headmaster of the school received £82 per annum, plus the school fees, which ranged from 2s 6d per quarter in the lowest classes to 5s in the highest. The fees covered reading, writing, arithmetic, geography, English, history and English grammar and composition; when Latin, Greek, French and mathematics were taught, an additional shilling was charged for each subject. But the teacher was always bound to teach gratuitiously twenty pupils selected by the Nicolson Trustees. In 1888, the school was handed over to the school board. In 1901, by a Decree of the Court of Session, its name, previously the Nicolson Public School, was changed to the Nicolson Institute. In 1898, the first boys went straight from the Institute to university, a trend that has not ceased since (see Chapter 8).

As far back as the turn of this century a recommendation was made for the provision of technical education on the island. A report on the subject of Higher Education in Lewis (1900) stated: 'Regarding the practical or scientific aspect of education . . . there is a clamant need of a central Technical School in Lewis . . . the local resources are quite inadequate for the establishment of such a school, or its maintenance, on an effective basis. Such popular technical instruction as Household Economy, Wood and Iron

Work, and Practical Navigation and Seamanship would be leading features.'

For many years afterwards technical education was available only on a voluntary evening-class basis. For instance, in September 1920 the Lewis School Management Committee offered evening classes in motor driving and maintenance, mathematics, dynamics, English, arithmetic and handwork in wood and metal. They were well supported and classes continued at sporadic intervals from that time. The plans for the present Lews Castle Technical College were passed in May 1948, after a lot of argument. Today the college has proved its worth; it is a centre of technical education in navigation and seamanship, weaving and textiles, building, engineering, and other pursuits important to the people of the Outer Isles.

In 1973 the Nicolson Institute received the Freedom of the Burgh of Stornoway, in recognition of the school's centenary which fell in that year. The event strengthened the 'town and gown' relationship which has always existed between the Burgh and the School, even more so today when the pupils participate in much of the social and cultural activity in the town.

4   COMMUNICATIONS

FROM the earliest times, the provision of communications in one form or another has been a matter full of incident and high colour. Gaelic folk-song contains many references to the hazards of crossing the impatient waters of the Minch. One such, a waulking song still known today, commemorates the death of Iain Garbh Mac Gille Chaluim, of Raasay in Skye, who was drowned in April 1617 on his way home from visiting the Earl of Seaforth in Lewis; it is said that he was drowned through the workings of his own 'muime', or foster-mother, who employed several famous witches to raise the tempest in which his ship foundered.

For well over a century the subject of adequate communications has aroused continuous argument. The strength of any island community lies in its ability to live within itself, while accepting the periodic injection of certain external items necessary for living or for work. A Londoner once expressed amazement at the isolation of Scarp, in West Harris, commenting that in Scarp they would not know what was happening in London. The indisputable rejoinder was 'Nor do they know in London what we would be doing in Scarp.' However, to a large island community, with a certain degree of economic significance, communications are the basic lifeline.

SEA ROUTES

When in the early 1800s formal sea communications were being established between the island and ports on the west coast of Scotland, down as far as the Clyde, most of the islanders were of course little affected. Except for the professional classes (merchants, ministers and the like), they had little use for the sea links provided for them. Their economy was not yet a cash economy, and travel was thus a luxury they could not afford. As the nature of local life began to change with the infiltration of some of the

64

trappings of nineteenth-century civilisation, however, they grew to depend on items brought by sea. Imported food, clothing, wood, metal domestic utensils and the like were slowly assimilated as indispensable everyday articles. But there was relatively little export in return; then as now, any transport operator struggled with the fact that traffic was one-way and the freight charges must pay for the double voyage. Though the fishing industry and later the Harris Tweed industry were, around the turn of the century, to do much to determine and stabilise shipping developments, both passenger and cargo services were always facing loss rather than profit.

On the social side of the picture, the regular call of ships to the island, to Stornoway in particular, was a welcome, quickening sign that the island was significant in some way to the outside world. The ships brought visitors who made the island, and the Hebrides in general, better known to other prospective travellers. The exposure of the island and its folk to the gaze of the mainland led to a wider knowledge and understanding which without doubt brought improvements in social welfare and a basis for economic development. When many islanders found it necessary to go to Glasgow and the south for work, the ships of the Minch served as a firm link with home, to which they returned whenever they could. This feeling for home is still manifest today in the Lewismen in Canada who charter an aircraft to Prestwick each year so that they can holiday on the island. Since 1900 or so, passenger traffic has been two-way : emigrants, migrants, visitors and business travellers. When the fishing industry was in its heyday, the ships carried hundreds of fisherfolk across the Minch to ports as far south as Great Yarmouth to 'follow the herring' round the shores of Britain and back to the Minch again. Traffic today is still considerable, with the air-link with the island being used to its capacity.

In a community where Sabbath observance is an integral strand of religious belief, ministers have on occasions tried to preserve the Mosaic sanctity of the Sabbath Day by restricting the movement of ships in Stornoway harbour. In deference to local feeling the Stornoway steamer has always docked for twenty-four hours over Sunday, to leave port for Kyle just after midnight.

This is only relaxed if emergency sailings are necessary. During the second world war attempts were made by Free Church ministers to stop the movement of ships in Stornoway harbour, but needless to say the war effort took precedence.

THE SHIPS

When Sir James Matheson bought Lewis in 1844, sea communications were still erratic: a mailboat or packet was running thrice weekly between Stornoway and Poolewe on Scotland's west coast. Sir James decided that a craft based on Stornoway would serve more efficiently both for general trade and for island-to-mainland transport, and he provided a regular steamer service. As this craft, the *Mary Jane*, was to carry mails, Sir James thought the Post Office should promote the service, and he struggled with that department for some years, eventually being promised a subsidy of £1,300. Though the scheme was to cost far more and had won no other financial support, the service began in 1846, Sir James being surety for the whole concern. He lost some £17,000. Another of his ships was the PS *Ondine*, which carried mails between Ullapool and Stornoway during the 1870s and '80s.

Quite apart from the Matheson ventures, things had been stirring in the south; the sea communications of the West Highlands and Islands were about to be commercially developed. One of the first ships on a regular run between Stornoway and the south was the *Ben Nevis*, a small wooden paddle vessel later to be wrecked south of Campbeltown in 1831 while homeward bound from Stornoway. G. & J. Burns was one of the main companies operating the early West Highland trade, managing to survive the vagaries of fortune until 1851, when its interests were passed to David Hutcheson, its chief clerk, on the condition that the Burns's nephew, David MacBrayne, became one of the partners. This was the beginning of the company so well known today, Messrs David MacBrayne Ltd. The new company started off with a building programme and gave birth to a long line of ships, many of whose names were to become bywords in the Western Isles.

The PS *Clansman* was the first. Her route was the strenuous one of Glasgow, Oban, Skye and Stornoway. Alexander Smith's

Summer in Skye gives a fascinating account, written from first-hand experience, of working conditions aboard. *Clansman*'s speed on her first voyage back from Stornoway was 13 knots; she was wrecked on Sanda Island after only fourteen years' service. The company's PS *Glencoe* was originally the *Mary Jane* built by Sir James Matheson for his Stornoway run, launched in 1846. In that year she plied from Stornoway to Portree, Tobermoray, Oban and Glasgow, with calls at Kyleakin, Balmacara and Armadale. She passed to MacBrayne's in 1857, was lengthened and with other alterations emerged for a long life of sea service, braving the terrors of the Minch waters as the saloon steamer *Glencoe*. Refitted with new engines during her lifetime, her first horizontal boilers were replaced in 1883 by others which, in 1901, were succeeded by a haystack boiler from the *Fusilier*. *Glencoe*'s original length was 150 ft, later extended to 165 ft; she was 20 ft broad and after her lengthening had a gross tonnage of 226. Her original machinery was a steeple, one-cylinder 56-in engine of 177 nhp. The end of the much-loved *Glencoe* came in the summer of 1931, when, despite the display of much sentiment, she was broken up at Ardrossan—after eighty-five years of service. When she died she was one of the two oldest working ships in the world.

The PS *Stork* was first built for Messrs Burns's Liverpool service and was later on the Belfast run. Acquired by Hutcheson's in 1858 she was placed on the Glasgow/Stornoway run with the *Clansman*, but in 1860 was sold to the Italian Government. Another brief encounter was the SS *Fingal*, which knew Stornoway for a few short months before being sold for the American Blockade, after capture becoming a Federal gunboat. Then came the SS *Clydesdale*, built in 1862 for the company by J. & G. Thomson and used on the Glasgow/Stornoway twice-weekly cargo and passenger service. She was 197 ft long, 24 ft broad and drew $13\frac{1}{2}$ ft of water; her gross tonnage was latterly 468. Her original engine (120 nhp) was a two-cylinder steeple (40 in—30 in); this was compounded in 1893, when she had a new double-ended boiler installed.

After the first *Clansman* came to grief on Sanda Island, a second ship of the same name was built for the Glasgow/Stornoway run. She was a most attractive two-masted iron ship, with a clipper bow, figurehead, and bowsprit with ornamental carving at both bow and stern. The *Clansman* left Glasgow every Monday and arrived back on Saturday mornings, a regular pattern maintained from 1870 to 1909. She was 211 ft long, 27 ft broad, with a draw of 13 ft of water, her engines having a nominal horsepower of 171; her gross tonnage was latterly 619.

The SS *Locheil*, two-masted with a straight stem and single funnel, in her early career ran the Stornoway mails from Ullapool, in the late 1870s. In 1884 she was fitted out for a three-months' cruise in the neighbourhood of Skye, a gunboat in attendance with a view to suppressing any riots likely to result from the then recently-initiated legislation introduced by the London Land Reform Association. She was also on the Dunvegan service, via Harris and Lochmaddy. In 1907 she ran aground at Portree and was afterwards broken up.

In 1879, David MacBrayne became sole partner and owner of the fleet of David Hutcheson & Co, and the name of the company was changed to David MacBrayne Limited. The first ship built for the fleet by MacBrayne was launched in July 1881 : the iron screw steamer *Claymore*. Her machinery consisted of a heavy two-cylinder compound engine supplied with steam from a pair of single-ended Scotch boilers; she never attained her full speed of 15 knots, at least not in service. She was 227 ft long, 29½ ft broad and drew 14½ ft of water. Her gross tonnage was latterly 776, and the indicated horsepower of her engines 1,400. She was sold in 1931 for breaking up. So high a regard did those on the west coast have for the *Claymore* that many parts of the ship went to places throughout Britain as souvenirs.

The PS *Great Western* was among MacBrayne's bought tonnage. This ship belonged to the GWR and spent most of her time on the Milford/Waterford route, though from 1878-85 she was transferred to Weymouth and ran across the Channel to Cherbourg. She came to northern waters as a straight-stemmed, two-masted, and two-funnelled cross-Channel steamer—both funnels being abaft the paddle boxes. MacBrayne placed her on the Stornoway mail service from Strome Ferry, which she maintained until being withdrawn temporarily in 1893 for a facelift in the MacBrayne standard design, emerging renamed *Lovedale*. She was returned to the Stornoway route and, on the extension of the Skye line of the old Highland Railway from Strome Ferry to Kyle of Lochalsh in 1897, the latter port became the southern terminus in the mail service to Lewis, as it still is. She was broken up in 1904.

Yet another ship with fond connections with Lewis folk was the SS *Shiela*, the second steamer of the new MacBrayne family. Both hull and machinery were the product of Inglis of Pointhouse, and she had the distinction of being the first steamer in the MacBrayne fleet to be fitted with triple-expansion engines. She was launched in January 1904, a fine-looking craft, named after a character in William Black's novel *A Princess of Thule*.

Though of only 280 tons, she fulfilled an important role for the Stornoway folk and their country cousins. Summer and winter, fair weather or foul for over twenty years *Shiela* carried passengers, cargo and mails between Kyle of Lochalsh and Stornoway. Purely a functional craft, she gave her many thousands of passengers a rough time crossing the Minch; but though she was often late—many times the seas and winds prevented any headway at all, though steaming to the limit—she never failed to make port. This Stornoway/Kyle route is the hardest-worked of all the MacBrayne fleet; a Minch crossing is made twice in every twenty-four hours, with a weekend rest of less than a day in Stornoway. The sturdy *Shiela* met a tragic fate : she deserved a better. Her regular Captain Cameron was away on leave, enjoying a few days' well-earned rest. The ship was in the hands of a temporary officer, who was not as familiar with the devious ways of West Highland waters as he should have been. Though the exact details of the accident are not available to the writer, it seems that the officer of the watch never saw the south Rona light on the inward passage from Stornoway in the early hours of Saturday, 1 January 1927. Thinking he had run his distance, he altered course with a view to making the Applecross call. He did not discover his error until too late and the *Shiela* ran aground in the darkness on the shores of Cuaig Bay, just south of Loch Torridon. No lives were lost, but the ship was a write-off.

From 1927 to 1929 Stornoway was served by a number of ships including the *Clydesdale II*, designed and built for the Glasgow/

Inverness cargo and passenger service, and the SS *Chieftain*. This latter was over 1,000 tons gross, with a clipper bow, single funnel, two masts, extensive passenger accommodation, triple-expansion engines, and silent-working electric winches.

In 1929, the TSS *Lochness* was put into commission for the Mallaig/Kyle/Stornoway mail service. Of 777 tons gross, and built of steel, she was 200 ft long, 34 ft broad and drew $10\frac{1}{2}$ ft. Her propelling machinery consisted of two sets of 150 nhp triple-expansion engines supplied by steam from single-ended, oil-fired Scotch boilers. These gave a full speed of about 14 knots. Many questions were raised in Parliament about the alleged inadequacy of the *Lochness* accommodation, particularly for third-class passengers, and the complaints led to the promise of a better ship. But the second world war intervened and it was not until 1945 that the *Loch Seaforth* (TMSV) was ordered. She was on duty in December 1947 and the *Lochness* transferred to the Islands route from Oban.

MacBrayne's mail contract of December 1938 stipulated that the company would provide two vessels, one to be for the Stornoway mail service. This proposed ship was delayed until 1945 when the order for *Loch Seaforth* was placed with Messrs Denny's shipyard. This vessel was the first of the MacBrayne fleet to be fitted with radar and was much larger than any of her predecessors on the Stornoway mail service. She had a gross tonnage of 1,089 and was 229ft in length. In 1972 the *Loch Seaforth* was withdrawn from the Stornoway service. Her place was taken by the *Clansman* ferry for a short period until the '*Iona*' took over to inaugurate a new ferry service between Ullapool and Stornoway rather than the traditional Kyle-Stornoway link. The facilities on the *Iona* for vehicles are good but the passenger accommodation is indifferent.

The first official hint of the coming of drive-on/drive-off car ferries for the Western Isles was made at the commissioning of David MacBrayne's *Loch Arkaig* in 1960. Under the Highlands and Islands Shipping Services Act, 1960, three vessels were built for the Secretary of State for Scotland, and were chartered by him to David MacBrayne Ltd for the new ferry services. One of these ships is the *Hebrides*, a twin-screw passenger and vehicle ferry

The Lewis village of Laxay on Loch Erisort

(*above*) Civil-engineering works in Lewis: the dam at the Gisla hydro-electric scheme

(*below*) Civil-engineering works in Harris: the Eilean Glas lighthouse on Scalpay Island, one of the four original lighthouses built in 1789. A new tower was built in 1824

vessel with a service speed of 14 knots. She can accommodate 600 persons (400 in winter) and over fifty cars, and has sleeping berths for fifty-one passengers. Powered by two supercharged diesel engines of Crossley make, she has a lateral-thrust propeller unit in the bows to aid berthing at piers, and is fitted with stabilisers. The MacBrayne colours have been used: black hull, red and black funnel, white superstructure and thin white waterline. The metal decking is painted a light green instead of the more usual brown or dark red. After completing her trials on the Clyde, *Hebrides* went into service on the Uig (Skye)/Tarbert (Harris)/ Lochmaddy (Uist) route on 15 April 1964. She was really a replacement of the *Lochmor* (of 1930), which had sailed across the Minch for almost thirty-five years, but which had many more ports of call, based at Kyle of Lochalsh and Mallaig instead of plying to and from the north of Skye. The Hebridean ferry berths at Tarbert and Lochmaddy on alternate nights, and spends the weekends at Tarbert. At the end of her first year of operation she carried nearly 11,100 vehicles.

SEA-RESCUE WORK

Closely associated with the sea services to the islands is the work of lighting the seaways and the rescue work which is at times required when the Hebridean seas are showing their teeth. The matter has occupied official attention for a very long time. Beginning at the northern tip of the island, the lighthouse at the Butt of Lewis is one of Britain's major manned stations. An oil-burning light was established there in 1862. In 1905 it was converted to an incandescent light, with a range of twenty-five miles. Three years earlier a fog signal was provided, and in 1930 a wireless beacon was set up at the station. At Tiumpan Head, at the tip of the Eye Peninsula, the light was established in 1900; it was oil-burning, converted to an incandescent six years later. The fog signal was not provided until 1959.

Eilean Glas lighthouse is one of the major manned lights which guide ships up the Minch. On the easternmost tip of Scalpay Island, in Harris, it was one of the four original lighthouses built by the Commissioners of Northern Lights in 1789. A new tower was built in 1824 with an oil-burning light, converted to incandescent in 1907. A fog signal was established in the same year.

The Arnish light is one of the first sights of Stornoway that welcome the island homecomer—and the last visible link when the island is left—so it has been duly celebrated in poem and song. Sited at the mouth of Stornoway Bay, it was established as an oil light in 1853, and in 1911 was converted to acetylene-gas operation. The keepers were withdrawn in 1963 and the light is now unwatched. Of the minor unmanned lights, Carloway is an acetylene-gas-burning light established in 1892; Greinam, on the shores of east Loch Roag, near Breasclete, was set up as an incandescent light in 1900. The light at Milaid Point, near Kebock Head on the east of Lewis, was established, with acetylene gas, in 1912; and the light at Rudh Uisenis, again on the east coast, a little south of Milaid Point, was an acetylene-gas burner set up in 1938.

But whatever the navigational aids, mishaps at sea still occur. The rescue services can help thwart the sting of death, not only for the islander but for the stranger craft feeling their way along unfamiliar, dark-night shorelines. The RNLI (Royal National Lifeboat Institution) station was first established in Stornoway in 1887, £1,000 being spent on building a lifeboat house and 140 ft launching slipway—launching was done by manual labour. The first lifeboat was the *Isabella*, costing £372 and the gift of a Mrs Duguid of London, a woman obviously true to her surname. The *Isabella* was launched only five times during her four years' service.

From 1901 to 1918, the *Sarah Pilkington* was launched five times and saved twelve lives from shipwreck. Then came the *Janet* (1918-24) which cost £810. She was launched only once, with no rescues. In the next four years the *James Marsh* saw no service; but the subsequent boat spent a busy quarter of a century (1929-54). She was the *William and Harriet*, built at a cost of £10,469; launched seventy-seven times, she rescued 130 lives, indicating the increase in sea traffic on the Minch and near waters. In 1954 her place was taken by the present lifeboat, the *James and Margaret Boyd*, then the largest type of lifeboat in the service until the building of 70 ft craft in 1965.

But neither is Harris behind in willing men. In December 1962 the trawler *Boston Heron* saw herself on off-lying rocks and broken surf water in a full south-westerly gale. The rock island of Stila-mair, off Scalpay Island, gave the stranded crew little hope of help. But six Scalpay men saw the plight of the ship and went out in a small open boat. Three of the trawlermen were saved, one of whom was found clinging exhausted to a rock. The other seven perished before more adequate aid could be brought. For their heroism, these Scalpay men were awarded Vellum Certificates by the RNLI. The attitude of local men to the sea, and the sea's treatment of men, was once summed up by an old Harrisman: 'Our men were brought up in the school that taught them that life was precious and that the soul was priceless.'

The formal organisation of sea rescue is found in the Coast-guard Stornoway, the headquarters of the Stornoway District. This covers the north-west coast of Scotland from Ardnamur-chan, Argyll, to Cailleach Head, the Minches and the associated sea areas, including the Small Isles, Skye and the Outer Hebrides —in all some 800 miles of coastline. The Stornoway station is base for a district officer, a station officer and four coastguardsmen, supported by locally-enrolled residents who form the Auxiliary Coastguard. Stornoway Coastguard is the launching station for the Stornoway and Barra lifeboats, advising when a launch is needed and calling out the boat crew by firing two green maroons. It is also a coastguard liaison station for the GPO Coast Radio Station (CRS) at Oban, and it co-operates with Oban and Wick as a radio-telephone station when lifeboats are launched on ser-vice. There is, in addition, liaison between Stornoway station and the RAF, the Royal Navy and Lloyd's: Lloyd's come into the picture when tugs, salvage and shipping information are required.

Though there have been many stranger ships and lives lost on and around the island's shores, local tragedies are not lacking. In December 1862 disaster overtook five boats from Port of Ness, out pursuing white fish. A fierce gale sprang up and the fishing-fleet perished, with thirty-one lives. Twenty-four widows, seventy-one orphans and thirty-one other dependents were left destitute, though they obtained some subsequent relief from a fund to which

Queen Victoria and the Prince of Wales, later King Edward VII, contributed handsomely. But that was only one item in a long chapter that will never close.

The most shattering disaster on Lewis shores was the loss of the *Iolaire* on the very last day of the year 1918. Before the New Year's Day of 1919 was a few hours old, over 200 sons and fathers were lying in the death-waters of their drowning, little more than a stone's-throw from their native island. Barely a village on the island was not affected by the sinking of the *Iolaire*, which was bringing soldiers and sailors back from the war to their homes. The subsequent findings of the Court of Inquiry are bald statements which convey nothing of the tragic loss of the cream of an island's male population in a matter of minutes. The jury found that the *Iolaire* went ashore and was wrecked on the rocks inside the 'Beasts of Holm' (outside Stornoway) about 1.55 on the morning of 1 January, resulting in the death of 205 men; that the officers in charge did not exercise sufficient prudence in approaching the harbour; that the boat did not slow down, and that the look-out was not on duty at the time of the accident; that the number of lifeboats, boats and rafts was insufficient for the number of people carried, and that no orders were given by the officers with a view to saving life; and, further, that there was a loss of valuable time between the signals of distress and the arrival of life-saving apparatus in the vicinity of the wreck. The sad affair is still remembered in the In Memoriam columns of the *Stornoway Gazette*.

AIR SERVICES

The people of the Outer Hebrides are among the most air-minded in the world. However, aeroplanes came late to the island. The first visit by an aircraft was in 1928, when Seaplane S1058 landed in Stornoway Harbour. The crew of five were treated to a luncheon by the town's civic heads. In 1932 the seaplane *Flying Cloud* arrived in the town, piloted by Lord Malcolm Douglas Hamilton. Owned by British Flying Boats Limited, it was the first commercial aircraft to land and caused some local talk about air services for the island. In June 1933 a large seven-seater aircraft belonging to the Midland and Scottish Air Ferries Limited came down at the golf course near Melbost; three or four attempts were made to land, but each time it touched down a small boy ran out to meet it and it was forced to rise again. The directors of the company were interested in establishing an air contact with the island. In September of the same year a giant RAF seaplane landed in Stornoway Bay, the S1589, the largest naval flying boat in the world at the time.

In 1933, Highland Airways Limited proposed an air link between Stornoway and Inverness. The following year, in March, saw the first commercial flight, piloted by an air pioneer in the north of Scotland, Captain E. E. Fresson. The service was intermittent, however. Then in September 1935 there was an agreement between the trustees of the Stornoway Estate and Captain Glyn Roberts of the West of Scotland Air Services Limited to establish an air service between Renfrew and Stornoway as soon as possible. The trustees gave this company the sole right to operate the service from the landing ground of Melbost golf course for a period of five years. Initially the service was to be thrice weekly, at £3 4s single fare. The interesting connection here was that Captain Roberts was the first man to operate an air mail service on behalf of the Canadian Government, along the route of the MacKenzie River, discovered by Stornoway's Sir Alexander MacKenzie; he carried mails to many of the settlements along the river which had previously been served irregularly. At the same time, survey flights over Lewis were being carried out by Captain Fresson of Highland Airways. These led to the construction of 600-yard runways at Melbost, with a radio station to be installed when the airport was complete.

In March 1938, the *Lochgarry*, an old cumbersome, single-screw vessel, was on the Stornoway run. When a sixty-mile an hour gale blew up she was unable to leave Kyle of Lochalsh. The Post Office, with commendable enterprise, chartered a Highland Airways plane to fly the mails from Inverness to Stornoway and return with island mails. But no regular air service for mails on this route was introduced until 1948. No special mark was introduced by the GPO, but first covers were marked 'First Lewis Air Mail, Feb 16th 1948. Stornoway to Inverness'.

COMMUNICATIONS

There were, of course, other types of flights before 1948. In 1937, Captain Fresson took the first sick person off the island on charter—the beginning of the air-ambulance service so valuable to the islanders. During World War II, certain RAF mails were flown between Glasgow and Stornoway, on which there were first covers (December 1943, Glasgow/Stornoway; December 1943, Stornoway/Glasgow; and January 1944, Glasgow/Stornoway). The present air services are supplied by BEA and Loganair Ltd. The BEA plane route is Glasgow/Benbecula/Inverness and return. Loganair offer a service Glasgow/Benbecula/Stornoway and return. In recent years this small firm has built up a most valuable inter-island air link.

OVERLAND ROUTES

The history of overland communications in the island is a short one, though it does, like American history, have many character-istic highlights. In early times getting from one place to another was simply a matter of following well-worn tracks across the moor-land, skirting lochsides and marshy lands and just taking the shortest distance possible between starting point and destination. Considering the length and breadth of the island, it is surprising that it was not until Sir James Matheson's appearance in Lewis that road-making was undertaken with any determination. This activity stemmed largely from the desire to get something in return for the outlay involved in keeping literal death from starvation clear of the doors of the island folk.

The report of the Rev James Headrick (prepared for Lord Sea-forth in 1800 and published about 1820) indicated that the pro-vision of roads would be of great benefit to the island. A footnote in the report (of probable date 1816) urges assistance from Parlia-ment or the Board of Fisheries to complete the road from Storno-way to Loch Roag, which had been begun by Lord Seaforth. There is a bitter complaint that though the Seaforth property bears a large share in the county assessment, 'not a penny of public money has ever been laid out in Lewis'. Another footnote records that the road from Stornoway to Aignish in the east was made in 1815. No large undertakings followed Mr Headrick's many recommendations, and though some road making began in 1791, progress was slow; in the course of fifty years, only 45 miles of road were created, less than a mile for each year. When Sir James Matheson took over in 1844 and planned to open up the island, he started with these 45 miles. On his death in 1878 there were more than 200 miles of road on which, with the necessary connecting bridges, he spent £25,593.

In the late autumn of 1882, a great gale swept away the hay and corn crops. This, added to the complete failure of the potato harvest, led to distress throughout the island. At a meeting called in Stornoway in December it was resolved that a memorial be forwarded to Mr Gladstone, then Prime Minister, craving aid from Government resources, or that some form of public works be started. No immediate response was made to this appeal. However, as the matter had been raised, investigations were made and eventually the Western Highlands and Islands (Scotland) Works Act, 1891, passed into law. It authorised, *inter alia*, the expenditure of a sum not exceeding £15,000 on constructing and improving the road between Carloway and Stornoway, and certain other roads approved by the Secretary for Scotland.

That Carloway was chosen as a terminus from Stornoway is significant. At the time it was probably the best fishing centre on the west coast of Lewis. Loch Carloway, which branches eastward from the mouth of Loch Roag, is a safe harbour and offers easy access; and any attempt to develop the real fishing potential of the district was a step in the right direction. At the time, the road from Carloway to Stornoway was a wandering one, 23 miles long, badly formed in many parts and ill-suited to heavy traffic. The proposed road was to be only 16 miles long and would, it was said, afford easy and quick access to Stornoway; fish would arrive there in fresh condition, suitable for transportation by boat to southern markets. As soon as the necessary plans were prepared and a contract drawn up, the work started. Progress was rapid, but financial difficulties arose. The contractor went bankrupt and the engineer was dismissed. The undertaking came to a complete standstill. Of the 16 miles, only 8 were completed. About 5 miles were partially made; the remaining 3 miles lay untouched.

The 1891 Act brought into existence a number of minor roads

and footpaths. Until this time, the greater part of the district of Park was accessible only on foot. Roads were 'at best rough narrow paths where rushes and grass grew between the tracks'. The Act improved the old *frith-rathad* (rough tracks) to such an extent that, says a report of 1902, 'a marked improvement has taken place in school attendance by their formation'. The opening up of the island certainly benefited the people. Though the moor tracks might give a more direct route to Stornoway, the roads at least offered a hard surface for horse-drawn cars and carts. The numbers of vehicles accordingly rose, and for long after the turn of the century the horse enjoyed a monopoly. Motor cars were beginning to be read about in the days-late newspapers brought to the island, but not until 1917 were the first complaints heard about cars tearing up the surfaces of the roads. Slowly but surely the inevitable pioneers emerged with their 'tin lizzies'. By 1925 there were an estimated 250 vehicles in Lewis—and traffic congestion was beginning to be a problem. The relative speed of cars was still something to be wondered at too : it was progress indeed to be able to travel from Ness to Stornoway and back again between a late breakfast and an early tea. But for all this progress, one could still buy a good dog-cart in excellent condition, to seat six people, for £9. A two-seater trap could be had for £6 10s; a set of harness cost 30s. And as for fuel—the best quality oats were 10s 6d per cwt. Indeed, it was not until 1943 that Stornoway Town Council sold its last horse—and only because no one could be found to look after it.

When Sir James Matheson came to Lewis in 1844 there was only one horse-drawn vehicle on the whole island. By 1872 eighty-seven wheeled vehicles were using his new roads. A pioneer of the wheel-carriage service, D. K. Henderson, began business in the 1850s. He was the first to carry mails and held a contract for the Stornoway to Tarbert run until the GPO introduced its own vehicles. As the motor took hold Henderson changed over and was the first to establish a motor-transport business on the island. Not all the local vehicles were of recognised makers' designs. A writer in the *Stornoway Gazette* in the mid-twenties commented on the fact that only the engine and the chassis of the local buses were imported. Bodies were then erected by carpenters . . . and boat-builders; many of the bodies were 'fearfully and wonderfully made', an understatement that did not go unnoticed by those who had to travel in the emergent public transport. Combined interests led to the formation of the Lewis Motor Owners' Association which agitated for better roads; existing highways were being pot-holed with alarming and uncomfortable rapidity to the detriment of their vehicles.

Very slowly did public transport become co-ordinated for the benefit of the travelling country folk. Routes were planned and approved. In 1932 there were daily tours for visitors to the island, a series begun by the late John Mitchell, a pioneer in the provision of bus services, with Stornoway as the 'Rome' of Harris and Lewis. In 1935 he was granted permission by the Traffic Commissioners to run daily services between Stornoway and Rodel.

The expansion of the Harris Tweed industry was responsible for developing transport, both for conveying yarn to weavers throughout the island and for mill-workers. In May 1933 John Mitchell began a suburban bus service for the people of Stornoway, though more for the conveyance of workers in the fish trade; tweed-mill workers and others were not slow to take advantage of it. In the following month, June, Mitchell ran a bus from Stornoway to the Market Place just outside the town at Bannadrove (Beinn na Drobh—hill of the market), for a 6d fare. In October of the same year, Peter MacAulay provided a twenty-seater Bedford bus for the Carloway to Stornoway run, and this vehicle was not a home-made affair. Meanwhile in Stornoway, a traffic census showed that, on average, 628 vehicles crossed Cromwell Street, the main thoroughfare, every day—and 799 pedal cyclists.

POSTAL SERVICES

Until the late years of the nineteenth century, the lack of postal facilities were not considered a great disadvantage : few people wrote letters.

The *Scots Magazine* in 1756 noted that 'A Post Office is to be established at Stornoway, in the island of Lewis, from the fifth of July next, with packet-boats for maintaining a regular communication with the mainland. The mail will be dispatched from Edinburgh every Thursday at eight o'clock at night, and should arrive at Edinburgh every Tuesday morning, but the arrival will sometimes be uncertain.' The development of a postal service in the hinterland of Stornoway was slow. In 1833 only one mail packet ran each week to Lewis, sailing from Poolewe to Stornoway, weather permitting (see Chapter 8), and the island still had only the one post office. By 1880, of course, more contact with the outside world was expected and there were eleven post offices in rural Lewis, with Stornoway's promoted to Head Office status. The latter had been for some time equipped with a money order and Savings Bank department. The telegraph had also been introduced, though no connection to any of the country offices existed; telegrams for all parts of the island other than Stornoway were, as a rule, forwarded by the first mail dispatched after the receipt of the message. By 1902 there were twelve telegraph offices in the country districts of Lewis (Harris was incommunicado with Stornoway, coming under the Inverness-shire arrangements). Some of these offices were set up under orders of the Highlands & Islands Work Board, the service being carried on by the Post Office without guarantee against loss. The office at Port of Ness was subsidised by the Fishery Board and Lloyd's, who had a signalling station at the lighthouse there.

Until 1926, when the long-universal red vans appeared, all mail was transported between the rural areas and Stornoway by private contractors, who used horses and latterly Albion coaches. A motor-launch operated between Callernish and Bernera; mails for South Lochs were conveyed across Loch Erisort from Crossbost to Cromore, and from Laxay to Kershader. In the early 1930s this area was served by mail van working between Stornoway and Lemreway. In 1950 full use was made of the existing BEA air service and, in order that mail from the rural areas could be included, additional main vans were outstationed at Lemreway, Callernish, and Port of Ness. These worked in to meet others working out from the town.

The Harris area was taken under the control of the head postmaster at Stornoway in 1937, having before this date been served by the head postmaster at Lochmaddy, North Uist. A mounted postman was at that time working between Tarbert and Flod-dabay, halfway down the east coast of South Harris. Before this transfer there was no direct mail link between Harris and Lewis. With the introduction of a bus service, a local mail was introduced between Stornoway, Tarbert and Leverburgh, and up to 1955 all mails for Harris were dealt with at Tarbert and Leverburgh, being dispatched to and received from mainland offices direct on a three-days-a-week basis. In 1955 a daily delivery service was introduced throughout Harris (with the exception of Scarp), all its mails being handled at Stornoway.

TELEGRAPH, TELEPHONE AND RADIO

The first telephone in Lewis was installed in 1897. The first telegraphic cable was laid in 1872; its continual breakdowns were a constant source of annoyance, particularly to local businessmen and fishcurers. Another cable for morse telegraph was laid about 1910, between Broad Bay in Lewis and Inverasdale on the Scottish mainland. This worked duplex to Aberdeen, the 'B' leg of the cable being used for an Inverness link. At about the same time, a morse-operated Stornoway-Lochmaddy-Castlebay (Barra) telegraph circuit was introduced which had to be balanced every morning before sending could begin. This was the last morse link in Scotland until its withdrawal in 1948. Though latterly it went only to Lochmaddy, originally it worked with one wire to Castlebay, Lochboisdale, and Lochmaddy, and thence to Tobermory and Oban. It was a four-wire circuit to Tarbert and single-wire to Castlebay; the batteries were housed in the attic of Stornoway Post Office. A new trunk telephone service between Lewis and the mainland began on 21 March 1933, celebrated by an inaugural call from the Provost of Stornoway to the GPO in Edinburgh. A four-core cable was laid between Loch Erisort and Staffin in Skye, complemented with some 25 miles of overland wire. It had to be balanced after every shower of rain! The first teleprinter was worked over this cable in the early 1930s. The use to which the fishing trade put the connection can be gauged by the fact that at the height of the fishing season up to 20,000 messages were handled each month. The first trans-Atlantic call came in

1935, when the Lewis Woollen Mills were called up by a Toronto mill.

Beam radio came in 1938-39 with two circuits. The stations were on Bennadrove Hill, outside Stornoway, and at Ullapool. In 1942 a twelve-channel link was opened to Gairloch. Outlying villages worked into Stornoway on single-wire circuits, with an earth return, Great Bernera being the last exchange to be served single-wire. One of the island's most remote inhabited satellite islands, Scarp, received its first telephone service only in 1947. Scarp was deserted by its native population in 1971.

The rate of increase in the use of telephone services in the island has been considerable. In 1965 some 1400 customers of the Post Office made almost 250,000 trunk calls. In 1972, the number of subscribers was 2,300. The projected number for 1975 is in the region of 3,500 subscribers who will make an estimated 500,000 calls per annum. In each case, the figure for local calls is very much higher. Every telephone exchange on the island has grown in size; of the twenty-one exchanges, the three largest are at Back, Carloway and Shawbost. In 1964 the Post Office set up a working party to examine the development of the telephone service in the Highlands and Islands. As a result of the party's report a scheme of improvement involving a capital expenditure of £7½ million will be spent on new buildings and access roads, exchange equipment, underground cables and radio equipment.

Stornoway has been provided with a new telephone exchange, and underground cables have been laid both in the town and in the outlying districts. Smaller exchanges in the country areas will have new equipment fitted. A modern radio system between Stornoway and Tarbert is being constructed. To link the island with the South, a new underground cable, costing £1 million, will link Inverness to Ullapool and Gairloch. It is estimated that by 1975 most townships in Lewis and Harris (the latter through a new Exchange building) will be on STD, at a cost of £500 for every connected subscriber in the island.

5   AGRICULTURE AND FISHING

THE economic possibilities of the peat blanket of the island, particularly in Lewis, have attracted the attention of many would-be exploiters. Sir James Matheson's advisers formed the idea that the Lewis hags could be turned to a good profit, and Sir James's series of peat reclamation and improvement programmes are still echoed today. He first cast his eye to the west, north of Achmore, a township set up more than a century ago on deep peat. The peat reclaimer he employed was none other than Alexander Smith, one of the best-known 'speculative' agriculturalists in Scotland at the time. Smith had already transformed the Carse of Gowrie from bog to a fertile tract of land; could he not do the same in Lewis? The site chosen was seven miles from Stornoway and the little hamlet established there was called Little Deanston, in recognition of Deanston, Perthshire, to which Smith belonged. The soil consisted of bog-moss, varying in depth from 3 to 8 ft. Sixty acres were wedge-drained and laid out in fields of ten acres enclosed with ditches and turf fences. Ploughing and trenching began and fertilizing agents were applied, including clay marl, shell sand, guano and dissolved bones. Two of the fields were put through a course of arable cultivation, the others being laid down in grass. After the fields had been worked for a few years it was found that the driest ground gave the best results. In time the land was handed over to some crofters from nearby Lochganvich, but in 1850 it was abandoned because of the difficulty in getting seaweed for manuring; and besides it was not possible to keep the land in good heart and to do fishing as well. The tract of land concerned today still shows a better quality of pasture than the adjacent natural moorland.

Smith gave his impressions voice in 1844, just after his first visit to Lewis, to the august members of the Glasgow Philosophical Society. The cultivation of the soil was as primitive as the islanders' manufacture of cloth. The inhabitants were at least a century behind the times, though they were, he found, in no way deficient by nature. They were social in their own style, and they had very good heads, 'that is, for people not accustomed to habits of thought'. So far as agriculture was concerned, nothing in the way of draining the land had ever been accomplished; nor had any effort been made to penetrate the hard sub-soil. He held that the great scarcity of timber had been a serious handicap when it came to agricultural implements—to their renewal, repair or possible improvement. Under direction, however, he was convinced that improvements in land use would result in considerable benefits to the island. He added that he hoped the period of this improvement would not be far off and that visitors would find 'a green, pastoral land instead of a dreary waste'.

Yet not until 1928 was peat reclamation and development again brought out for an airing. This time, the benefactor was the late Mr T. B. MacAulay, a Montreal magnate, a son of Lewis connections. He gave £10,000 to establish an experimental farm in Lewis, and a site on Arnish moor, not far from Stornoway, was chosen. It was typical of most of Lewis: black, water-holding peat, which when squeezed, instead of allowing water to escape from it like a sponge, oozes itself through the fingers. The aims of the farm were to provide additional arable land on which to grow winter fodder, and to improve, at as low a cost as possible, the grazing on the moorland. Fifty acres were certainly converted from moorland to arable, and this formed a basis for an experimental extension to another 100 acres. By 1936 the farm had a sales income from produce of about £1,400. The stock in that year included 40 head of thriving cattle, including 15 dairy cows, 20 poultry, 140 blackfaced sheep, and some fattening pigs. The sheep were a late addition, made with the dual aim of pasturing on moorland too deep and soft for cattle in wet weather, and of improving the sheep strain of the island.

By 1938, it had been shown that some lasting improvement on moorland of reasonably favourable slope could be effected at a materials cost of about £3 per acre, and without heavy labour costs. Thus, the common grazings held by the crofting townships could be improved, if a co-operative effort were organized. So far as the reclamation of arable land from moorland was concerned, however, requiring as it did under-draining and cultivation, the labour costs were heavy, approaching the £20 per acre mark including the liming and fertilizing.

Though the farm was used for dairying with some reasonable results, the moorland acres put into good heart at Arnish were left to deteriorate. The run-down of the experiment followed the depression of 1933. Funds dried up, and in 1939 the farm was let to a tenant. But the lesson obtained from the MacAulay farm was a good one. By simply dressing with shell sand, of which large quantities are available on the shore-lands, applying some form of phosphate and seeding with cheap clover or ryegrass—involving no cultivation—large areas of moorland can be persuaded to do a good job. The work at present being undertaken by crofters to improve moorland grazing is worth mention. Areas of land have been given a surface application of approved compound fertilizers, phosphates, lime or shell sand, and selected grass-seed mixtures. The results are literally a sight for sore eyes, and bring Alexander Smith's 'green, pastoral land' close to realisation. Although individual crofters have taken advantage of the help given to regenerate rough grazings, the most spectacular results have been seen on the township common grazings; most of these have been fenced off and improved. Today, something like 14,000 acres of lush green pastures are steadily spreading over deep peat where formerly grew only sedges and brown heather.

To end this aspect of land use in Lewis on a historical note, the story of re-seeding had its beginnings during the time of the Napoleonic Wars. A minister who had some land at Barvas, on the west coast of the island, decided to attempt the reclamation of useless heather-bound and bracken-choked land. He sanded the area with shell sand, seeded it with a good strain of grass and used sheep to tamp in the seed. One can imagine what Lewis would be like today if the Barvas minister's work had been followed up by Alexander Smith and those who set up the farm at Arnish.

The pursuit of agricultural processes, their growth, development and improvement, to establish a foundation for a secure society has never been easy on the island. The unyielding nature of the base rock, Archaean gneiss, its hardness, its non-porous property, have all contributed to the resultant pattern and character of society which emerged. Though one is tempted to define crofting as an agricultural activity, it is also something much more intangible: a way of life. To quote the Napier Report on *The condition of the crofters and cottars in the Highlands and Islands of Scotland* (1884): 'Habit and local affection bear so great a sway in the actions of mankind, that Highlanders will be found who would rather be proprietors in the mountains of Skye, or the wastes of Lewis, than on the fertile plains of Manitoba.' 'There is the Island of Lewis, with poor, peaty soil covering the Archaean gneiss, but with a crowded, lively, vivid community,' said the Taylor commision in 1955 (Commission of Inquiry into Crofting Holdings).

The Highland crofter is the subject of an extensive literature. A special authority, the Crofters Commission, exists solely for the purpose of caring for his needs. He has special rights and privileges which are safeguarded by the Land Court. Crofters' unions have formed themselves into a strong federated wall for the system's defence.

Socially, the term 'crofter' means, on the island at any rate, a landholder who cultivates his own (arable) holding, his croft. He shares the common pastures with his fellow-crofters, each of whom has a right to carry a sum of so much stock, the 'souming'. These common pastures or grazings are a social link of some considerable significance, forming the basis for the crofting township, as distinct from the communities set up under the influence of some agricultural land use such as hamlet or village, where there are both small-holders and true farms, and the only communal land is the village green or common. For instance, outside the crofting counties area the main unit of Scots life in the country is the farm, with its tied cottages. Then come the full-time small-holdings important in the north-east and the southern Highlands.

Two Stornoway scenes from the 'Grand Collotype Album of Views in Lewis' published c 1900 by Samuel Lawrence, 'Chemist, Druggist, Perfumer, Stationer and Tobacconist', Cromwell Street, Stornoway. (*above*) The herring fleet in Stornoway harbour, showing the wherries or 'Zulu' type craft; (*below*) Cromwell Street

The inner harbour at Stornoway, taken from Gallows Hill. Lews Castle, now the Lews Technical College, is seen on the left. The trees of the Castle policies were planted by Lady Matheson

EARLY AGRICULTURE

In the past the land was worked with reasonable efficiency, at least to produce a subsistence economy. The reports of various observers on the islander point to this. But they also record a slow deterioration in the use of land with an agricultural element, as distinct from crofting. First, to Donald Monro, Dean of the Isles. His account of the Western Isles (*c* 1549) indicates that the population was very much greater then than now, and methods of agriculture were not far behind those used on the mainland. In addition to the raising of cattle, cereal crops were grown. Harris was 'very fertile and fruitfull of corne store and fisching, twisse mair of delving in it nor of teilling'. Lewis was 'faire and waill inhabit at the coste, ane fertile fruitfull countrey, for the most part all beire [barley] . . . in this ile ther are many shiep, for it is verey guid for the same.' Taransay (on the west of Harris) is reported as 'ane rough ile with certain tounes weil inhabit and manurit; but all this fertill is delved with spaides excepting as meikell as ane horse pleuch will teill and zet they have maist abundance of beir, meile of corne, store and fishing.' One must, however, regard the Dean's account in the light of his mission, which was to visit the Hebrides in a pastoral capacity. His concern was thus chiefly with Church lands which, agriculturally speaking, were the best. There is evidence also that the clergy in the islands were as good farmers as they were theologians and, as elsewhere, stimulated agriculture by example and precept.

The next reporter was Captain Dymes, sent from London *c* 1630, to report on the islanders, their agriculture and their ways of fishing. He confirms much of what the Dean said, even though one suspects that a pinch or two of adjectival seasoning has been added, for was not King Charles interested in Lewis and its resources? Again Lewis is described as 'very profitable and fertile alswell of corns as all kinds of bestiall wild fowl and fishes and specialie of beir sua that thair will grow commonlie 20, 18 or at leist 16 bolls beir yeirlie after ilk bolls sawing'. Harris was 'fertile, commodious and profitable in all sorts'.

About half a century later (*c* 1695) Martin Martin paints a different picture. Agriculture is in a shameful state of neglect and conditions backward. He tells us that the Island of Lewis had been fruitful in corn until late years of scarcity and bad seasons. The crops were barley, oats, rye, flax and hemp. The natives showed great industry in digging the ground with spades—a practice which he invariably associates with a large return. He even records that the abundance of corn had once been such that it encouraged them to 'brew several sorts of liquor'. For manure, sea-ware and soot were used. And harrows had two rows of teeth and rough heather in the third row. Pennant's visit to the island in 1772 found that the produce of the land was insufficient to support the population. Distress was rife.

In Martin's time, although the economy was more or less self-sufficient, a certain amount of produce was available for export or for translation into 'several sorts of liquors, as common usque-baugh, another called trestarig id est, three times distilled, which is strong and hot.' One assumes that this produce was surplus to the requirements of the island's population. The livestock consisted of 'cattle, horses, sheep, goats, and hogs'.

TACKSMEN AND TENANTS

Most of those who held land had leases: tacksmen, who paid rent for large tracts of land and who, by settling suitable tenants there, received rents, in money or in labour, as an additional income from their farms. These smaller tenants had no leases: they could not write and were subject to the tacksman's favour. In the early eighteenth century, the rental rolls for Lewis, preserved among the Seaforth Papers in the Register House in Edinburgh, show that most of the tacksmen—sixty-four in number—were MacKenzies, indicating that they were adherents of the Seaforth (MacKenzie) family on the mainland, who had received the lands from royal hands as the reward for their fidelity. The smaller tenants, who generally lacked surnames but were known by their personal characteristics, numbered over 200; there were also above eighty tenants in Stornoway.

Rents were paid either in money or, more often, in meal, mutton, sheep, butter, tallow or salmon. When it was proposed to sell the Seaforth estate of Lewis in 1772, particulars of the Lewis

rental were published for the benefit of intending purchasers, a
value in sterling being placed on the items :

Money	£713	3	3
Oatmeal, 256 bolls	89	2	2
Sheep, 228	25	6	8
Butter, 173 stones	28	19	7
Tallow, 7 stones	1	3	4
Salmon, 1 barrel	3	0	0
Total =	£860	15	0

The most important event in the agricultural history of the
island at this time was the introduction of the potato. Though the
exact date is not known, some evidence from the writer on Lewis
in the *Old Statistical Account of Scotland* (1796) places it about
1757. 'With the utmost difficulty . . . the people were prevailed
on to plant potatoes, but of which they now plant great quantities
by the plough and by the spade, and find them to be the most
useful of all crops raised in the Parish.'

The substantial tacksman seemed, in Lewis, to deal kindly with
those who called him Fear Baile (Town Man—almost a mayor,
without the trappings and self-elected). Serious complaints against
tacksmen are few. But winds of change were blowing. John Mac-
Kenzie, who had for some years been Chamberlain of the Lewis
Estate, was examined before the Napier Commission in Edinburgh in 1883. He knew the island's history well.

Till the beginning of this century, the greater part of the Lewis
was in the hands of tacksmen, or middlemen, who got in some
cases from their sub-tenants in money, produce, and labour what
nearly paid their rents. There were the MacIvers of the Parish of
Stornoway, the Morisons and Murrays of Barvas, the MacAulays
of Uig, and the MacLeods of Lochs. When Mr Stewart-MacKenzie
married the Hon Lady Hood, daughter of Lord Seaforth, and
took the management of the estate into his own hands, he did
away with the middlemen and let the land directly to the crofters.
This, no doubt, was a step in the right direction, but it had its dis-
advantages, as the example of a good middleman, who looked after
his people, and who was industrious in farming and attentive in
stock-breeding, was beneficial to the people, though in some cases
they may have been petty tyrants.

With the disappearance of the middlemen, their sub-tenants became tenants of the proprietor; and the descendants of these are most of today's crofters. Mr Thomas Knox, who became Chamberlain of Lewis in 1833, was examined before a Select Committee of the Houses of Parliament on the question of emigration from the island in 1841. At that time there were 1,913 small tenants on the island who paid yearly rents varying from 63s 9d to 72s 3d. He stated that the country produced sufficient corn for the use of the people in most seasons. The years 1836-7 were exceptional and outside relief became necessary. But he did not consider that any person in Lewis was poor who had a lot of land, however small, if it were sufficiently stocked. There were, however, in the island, small tenants occupying land unsuitable for raising grain; and in order to avoid such distress as had occurred in recent years he had advocated the emigration of about 6,000 people, the vacant ground to be put under sheep. This course had been followed in 1838, when five families numbering about seventy people were removed and the land they had occupied was converted into sheep farms.

In the end, however, only a small fraction of the proposed 6,000 persons ever left Lewis under Knox's scheme. Those who were left worked their land under a cloud of increasing distress, in a system which had them in an iron grip. Eventually the bubble burst, as indicated in Chapter 3. The pressure of social conditions, and the events of historical progress, were manifested first in the social action against the agricultural system and finally in the legislation which gave the crofter certain rights.

CROFTING CHANGES

In general, the island during the last century was able to support its population, failing to do so only when disease struck at the staple potato. Each family unit in the crofting township was self-sufficient in most grown produce and the milk products from the family cow. Very poor families grew potatoes only and depended on neighbours for milk. But when the potato crops failed, distress knocked at almost every door, the fishing communities on the island tending to relieve hunger by looking to the sea. The removal of crofters from good to poorer ground was a significant factor in the destitution years of the nineteenth century, with the self-sufficiency factor becoming smaller and the dependence on imports (when there was money to buy these) increasing. Today, the crofter is of course not self-supporting, his economy being based on fishing and weaving with the produce of the croft yielding an annual average of some £200.

Acreages under certain crops show this trend to dependence on the produce of mainland farmers. In the island in 1911 some 3,673 acres were under potatoes, the present acreage being about one-third of that. The number of people per acre of potatoes for Scotland as a whole is 22 : 1. In the island it is about 15 : 1, indicating a heavy domestic consumption. Yet substantial imports of this crop are required to satisfy demand; a relevant point is that the milking cow commonly shares the potatoes. The barley crop, once much used in Lewis's former small distilleries, has been reduced to some 10 per cent during the past fifty years. On the other hand, the acreage of sheaf crops, oats, rye and mixed corn, generally fed to cattle, has about doubled. Oats in particular are in favour for cattle fodder; even before the turn of the present century oats were not widely used for human food, and oatmeal has for centuries been imported into the region. The turnip acreage has halved over the past fifty years, perhaps the result of the gradual disappearance of the horse, its steady labour and its dung being required to put good heart in to the land.

As the crofters' cropping policy has changed over the past half century, so has their animal husbandry. Animals are a main selling product, particularly cows and sheep. Horses, of course, have been drastically reduced from their total of 1,672 in 1911, as tractor, lorry and van have taken over their work. And though some cattle are raised, the numbers are now about 60 per cent below those of 1911. At that time the density of cattle per 1,000 acres was heavy (46-60) in the north-east of Lewis, less (31-45) in the north-west, and still less further south. The present average is around 18 beasts per 1,000 acres. This decline, in particular in the milk-yielding animals, has compelled Lewis to import 1,000 gallons of milk a day from the mainland.

It is sheep which today claim pride of place on the croft, valued for mutton and for wool, the right type for translation into Harris Tweed; the predominant breed is the blackface, whose fleece is hard, wiry and long-lasting. The demand for raw wool has also encouraged larger flocks among crofters in such places as Barra, where virtually no weaving is done in the immediate locality. In general there has been since 1911 a 40 per cent increase in the livestock carried on the island's crofts, about twice as big a rise as found anywhere in the seven crofting counties of Scotland.

In an attempt to reduce Lewis's milk imports, in 1962 three crofters at Garrabost on the Eye Peninsula combined to set up a small dairy farm using the lands of their three crofts. A new dairy byre and dairy premises were built and equipped with the necessary electrical equipment. Grants were given by the Department of Agriculture & Fisheries for Scotland, the Crofters Commission, and the Highland Fund Limited. The first year of operation was closely supervised by the Lands staff of the Department at Stornoway and guidance given as necessary. The milk is retailed in Stornoway and district and amounts to about 5 per cent of Lewis's daily consumption. This little scheme has shown that the island could with some organised effort become independent of milk imports, which have been estimated at upwards of £100,000 worth per annum. Over £70,000 per annum is also spent on imported butter and cheese.

In 1947 the number of crofts in Harris and Lewis was 4,020. In 1971 the figure was 4,146 (3,592 being in Lewis), representing a slight increase in a quarter of a decade. Thus, crofting as a land use activity in the island provides a fairly stable element in the economy, although it is subsidised by the crofters' participation in the fishing and tweed industries. A crofter, it should be mentioned, is often a tenant of more than one croft, working them together as a unit. These units vary in size, the greatest bulk of them (about 60 per cent) having up to 5 acres of arable land. About 2 per cent contain over 30 acres of arable land. In recent years there have been proposals for the better use of the reclaimed moorland, particularly for cattle-raising, which would offer the crofter an increased cash yield from his interests. The annual reports of the Crofters Commission indicate, indeed, that the trend to the small croft obtained from the fragmentation of larger and more economic working units of over 30 acres of arable land is also apparent in the southern Hebrides, the west mainland of Ross & Cromarty, Argyll (mainland and islands) and Caithness.

The acreage of common grazings held per holding varies from under 50 to some 200. The crofts, as already mentioned, are in townships, of which the island has 168, half being fenced and half consisting of individually fenced crofts. During the winter most of the crofts are laid open for winter grazing by sheep of general ownership. Manure resources are mainly dung, seaweed, shell sand and of course artificials where necessary.

A new aspect of crofting in Lewis is its extension into forestry. A recent survey by the Forestry Commission indicated that under 400 acres of the land not being used for crofting were suitable for afforestation, and that these acres were made up from twenty-three different plots. At Garynahine Estate can be seen the beginnings of a real afforestation unit of some 500 acres, a scheme of the utmost significance for the economic future of Lewis and for the relationship between crofter and landlord. Too often in the past this relationship has been biting, hard and inflexible; in particular the crofter was understandably unwilling to release good land for planting trees. But the crofters of Callernish agreed that the right of usage of 285 acres of the common grazings belonging to their township should revert to the landlord, this land being thrown in with 220 acres of the Garynahine Estate. Labour comes from the affected township and others in the area.

FISHING

Early beginnings

It is the humble herring that has contributed so much to the island's economy and its history. At a very early date in history, the Hebridean fishings were worked by Frenchmen and Spaniards who must have found them rich enough to repay the long journey and weeks away from home in the cold Minch waters. It was not, however, until the end of the sixteenth century that the wealth of the Minch was really discovered, this time by the fishermen on the mainland of Scotland who copied the tricks of their trade

97

from the enterprising Dutch. Dutch fishing-busses were constantly off the island coast as early as the reign of James V. In 1594 the Hollanders made their first recorded visit to Lewis; they had a licence from Scotland's James VI which allowed them to fish outside a limit of twenty-eight miles.

It was, indeed, partly the success of the Dutch fishings which attracted the Gentlemen Adventurers of Fife, backed by the King in their unsuccessful endeavours to colonise Lewis. James VI's son, Charles I, was similarly enticed by the Minch, proposals being put forward for the purchase of Lewis by the Crown and for the formation of a new corporation, under English auspices, which would develop the island's fisheries. The corporation, founded in 1633, was the 'Company of the General Fishery of Great Britain and Ireland' and its main seat of operation was to be in Lewis. As Lord Seaforth was owner of the island at the time, he was invited to join the company's board, so that he could, with his influence, 'keep the islanders in awe'. One of the fishing stations set up in the Hebrides was on the island of Hermetray in the Sound of Harris. Martin Martin, writing of this island at the close of the same century, says that he saw 'the foundation of a house built by the English, in King Charles the First's time, for one of their magazines to lay up the cask, salt, etc, for carrying on the fishery, which was then begun in the Western Islands; but this design miscarried because of the civil wars which then broke out.' The scheme indeed fell flat (in 1640), and though Charles II tried to revive it on a commercial basis, lack of capital caused it again to come to nothing.

Where were the islanders in all this activity to develop the fishings around them? Strangely, there was a definite disinclination to fish until the Dutch, by their example, illustrated how fish could become a new factor in their economy. Lord Seaforth was vitally interested on his own account. When he acquired Lewis (in 1610) he set about establishing what amounted to a principality quite independent of recognised authority; and in contravention of the laws and privileges of Royal Burghs, he set up Stornoway as a fishing port, introducing a number of Dutch fishermen to prosecute the fishings in the Minch. In 1629, the Commissioners of Royal Burghs complained to the Privy Council of Lord Seaforth's conduct in this matter. They alleged that he 'draiv in hither an number of strangers who daylie resorts to and fra Holland to the Lewes and continent next adjacent (the Ross mainland presumably) and has caused them be answered of all such commodities as these bounds affords, as nameli with fishes and beeves quhilkis with the hyde and tallow, with manie utheris commodities they transport to Holland.'

To satisfy the Royal Burghs, Seaforth had some of his Dutch friends sent away. But several Dutch families remained in Stornoway until the outbreak of hostilities between England and Holland in 1653.

In Harris, similar efforts were promoted by Captain Alexander MacLeod, who in 1779 bought Harris, together with St Kilda, for £15,000 from the commissioners acting on behalf of General Norman MacLeod. The latter had, in 1772, inherited from his grandfather both the chiefship of Harris and a debt on the property amounting to some £50,000. Captain MacLeod, who skippered the East Indiaman *Mansfield*, did much to stimulate better conditions in Harris, and advocated the generation of a fishing industry. In the face of opposition and ridicule he showed by practical example what could be done to make a success of the herring fishings, introducing a number of east-coast fishermen with Orkney trawls to teach the inhabitants, and reaping a good harvest from the fishings off Rodel, despite the dismal auguries uttered by the Harris-folk. He improved the local harbour accommodation and erected a storehouse for salt, casks and the like, he built a factory for spinning woollen and cotton thread, and twine for herring-nets; he advanced money to those fishermen who were interested for the purchase of boats and gear; and he provided them with rent-free cottages with a ground-patch on which they could grow potatoes. He built roads between the village of Tarbert and the two jetties he made there, and he erected a schoolhouse and an inn. But all this hard work to put Harris on some realistic economic basis came to little. The native population were slow to appreciate the potential income lying about them.

The potential of the sea was of course eventually realised, particularly where the fishing grounds were favourable, Stornoway and its neighbourhood becoming the centre of the growing industry. In 1793, the Lewis Parish contributors to the *Old Statistical Account of Scotland* indicated that upwards of 183 boats were fishing off the island. In Uig no less than 275 netmakers were recorded, showing that the fishing industry was prosecuted with some measure of enthusiasm. 'All the people dwell in little farm-villages and they fish in the summer season. The women do not fish; but almost at all times when there is occasion to go to sea, they never decline that service, and row powerfully.' In the parish of Barvas in the eighteenth century some 9,000 Scotch pints of oil were taken each year from dog-fish livers and sold to Stornoway merchants at from 6d to 8d per pint; it is related that the tenants of Ness were able for a long time to pay their rents with the oil proceeds. Cod and ling were the principal fish caught by the men of Lochs, an annual average of 24 tons being cured and sold in Stornoway. Generally, other fish caught were consumed locally.

Loch Roag on the west of Lewis proved to be about the best fishing ground; in 1794 about '90 sail' from all parts of the United Kingdom were at the herring fishing there. At one time Loch Roag-cured herring was exported exclusively to Sweden. The minister of Stornoway, contributing to the *Old Statistical Account*, gives figures showing the quantities of fish shipped from the port from 1791 to 1796. During these six years some 14,000 barrels of herring were exported to the Continent, and 20,000 sent for consumption in Britain; some 350 tons of cod and ling were destined for Continental markets. Herring, cod, and ling were thus pursued during the following years with growing vigour, though the inshore white fish took favour. The herring fishing did not make great strides, mainly because to the middle of the nineteenth century catches were confined to the inland sea lochs; the people for the most part were not familiar with deep-sea fishing, and their boats and nets were not suitable for it.

Indeed, when Sir James Matheson bought Lewis in 1844, he gave scant attention to the potential in the fishings round his island. Though he expended considerable amounts in securing a regular steamer communication between the mainland and the island, and spent over £2,000 in building a quay at Stornoway for the steamers, he thought that any improvements in connection with the fishing industry should be paid for largely by the fish-curers themselves—though he did spend about £1,000 on constructing fish-curing houses. Why Sir James, with his experience of business, should have taken this attitude is not clear; certainly the fishing industry could have been given just the right impetus with his interest, personal and financial. As it was, the industry was left to develop on its own lines, with odd injections from time to time.

Fluctuating prosperity

That the potential in the fishing grounds of the Minch was enormous was realised before 1850 by fish-curers from the Scottish mainland. But deep-sea-going boats were needed, and so new designs were called for. James Methven of Leith, a pioneer of deep-sea herring fishing, sank capital into the development of a large class of boats known as the 'Anstruther build', or in the islands as 'Eanstrach'. These craft served the islanders well, and Lewis prospered, as did Stornoway. In the five years 1870 to 1875, for example, the average number of barrels of herring cured at Stornoway for export was some 80,000. From 1875 to 1900 the average Stornoway district catch of white fish, much of it caught by local boats and some of it cured at Carloway, was worth over £100,000; it was sent to Ireland and the Clyde. After 1900, fresh-trawled fish replaced the cured and the market fell away. In 1921, the market value of cured fish from Stornoway was about £500, $\frac{1}{2}$ per cent of the 1900 value.

The herring fishing held its own, against the decline of the white fish. Stornoway, as Lochboisdale in the Southern Isles, became for a while one of the world's most important fishing ports. Prosperity was in the air; even when the fishings did eventually fall away, there still remained, decades later, the whiff of past success among the neglected curing sheds, the hangdown boats in the quays, and the silent kippering houses. From 1917 to 1935, the annual landings of herrings (in crans) varied from 25,486 (in 1934) to 221,519 (in 1927). In that year, a record one, it was reported that 'even landsmen could hear the roar of herrings in Loch Erisort. So dense were the shoals that their progress in the water could be heard on shore.' Yet cash returns were poor: demand was falling off as foreign markets organised their own fleets, and the Scottish fishing industry as a whole was not commercially efficient. In 1936 landings were 40,829 crans; in 1937, 31,969.

From about 1850, Stornoway had begun to see the nucleus of what was to be a great fishing fleet in its harbours; but it had

A 'Zulu', a type of old fishing wherry used in Lewis at the turn of this century

something of the sort much before then. A pamphlet on the fishing industry published in 1790 tells us that the trade of the Stornoway merchants began to grow after the Union of the Parliaments in 1707, when Scottish herring were first admitted to the English colonial market. 'Some twenty-five or thirty years ago, all the fish they caught were carried for them to their port of destination by hired vessels. Now they can show in their own harbour, in the fishing time, upwards of thirty sail of stout handsome vessels, from 20 to 70 tons burden, all their own property.'

Towards the turn of the nineteenth century, the number of

herring boats belonging to Lewis was about 165, reaching a peak of 197 in 1889; the number of boats used for cod and ling fishing reached a peak of 704 in 1895. The figures, however, fluctuate considerably from year to year. The main reason for this was probably that these boats were not personally owned, but largely belonged to fish-curers and businessmen, to whom the boat crews were in debt, having received capital advances from them and from the State for boats and gear. Crews who had bad luck at the fishing had their boats impounded and sold to recover the amount of the loan. Many boats were also wrecked, for navigation in bad weather is still difficult even in these days of advanced directional aids.

The state loans to fishermen are worthy of note here, because they foreshadowed a similar scheme in the 1960s. They were made under the Crofters Holding Act 1886. Section 32 of the Act authorised the Fishery Board for Scotland to make advances, by way of loan, to persons engaged in the prosecution of the fishing industry, whether crofters or others in crofting parishes. For new boats, the maximum sum advanced was £312. The loans carried an interest of $3\frac{1}{2}$ per cent; repayments of principal and interest were over a period of from four to ten years. Loans for the improvement of existing boats were also advanced, varying according to the condition of the boat or other circumstances affecting the necessary security requirements. New boats were mortgaged to the Fishery Board.

Ninety-three Lewis fishermen received loans totalling some £12,000, and a sum of £18,000 was distributed in loans throughout all the crofting counties. In a report issued in 1901, it was indicated that these ninety-three Lewis fishermen had repaid about 82 per cent of their principal and interests, but in other counties the repayment percentage was under 60 per cent. The Lewis figure would have been higher were it not for the loans made to the Barvas fishers, on which the repayment figure was only 24 per cent. When borrowers failed to observe their part of the contract the Fishery Board seized the boats. Many of these loans were originally made to aid a deserving class of men in adverse circumstances and surroundings. To achieve the high overall percentage of repayment (some indeed managed to pay off all their debts) much hard work was called for, as well as skill in locating herring shoals. The seasonal migration of herring is still a puzzle to marine biologists; it contributed to many a Lewis fisherman drawing a blank, to his ruin, while his neighbour came home flushed with success.

The financial values of the fishings of the island, particularly Lewis, are some index to its fluctuating prosperity. In a *Guide for Scotland*, intending visitors to Stornoway were told that the annual figures for herring exports were, in 1860, some £60,000; for cod and ling, £13,600; smoked haddocks were valued at £1,600; lobsters at £1,396. Herrings caught in Harris and Lewis in 1889 were valued at £57,071. Two years later, the figure was £90,738, but after that year it steadily declined to reach a little over £20,000 in 1894. Increasing again, the catch in 1898 was valued at £128,707. There was a subsequent decline, picking up a little at irregular intervals, which continued until the effective demise of the industry just before the second world war, that is so far as Lewis was concerned. These catches of valuable herrings were not made solely by Lewis boats; the catches of many stranger boats, from the east of Scotland, must also be taken into account, to leave about 20 per cent as direct return to the island.

In 1938, the total catches of herring amounted to £98,000 for fresh fish and £162,400 for cured herring. This catch was obtained by 111 steam-drifters, five of which were locally registered at Stornoway, and some motor-boats, of which one-third were strangers. Harris has never been particularly prominent in the herring-fishing industry; shell fishing has been more profitable. In the years just before 1900, the average annual value of shell-fish caught in Harris was £2,306, only £500 below the Lewis figure. The Harris proportion of the aggregate herring and white-fish returns in the same period was just over £17,000, compared with the Lewis figure of £1,137,000.

Since the second war

Just before the second world war, Stornoway Fishery District furnished some 10 per cent of the Scottish cure of herrings, which averaged well over half a million barrels in 1937 and 1938, valued at about £1,500,000. Of demersal (sea-bottom) fish, the District furnished less than 1 per cent of Scottish landings. The war's aftermath brought too many changes for the island to cope with. Markets had disappeared; food habits had changed; capital was scarce; and many ex-servicemen saw the writing on the wall for fishing as a full-time activity. Also, many sea-going crofters of the pre-war fishing fleet were now dead, memories on fading photographs. Nor had the Western Isles fisheries ever fully caught up with those of the main fishing bases of Britain and the east coast of Scotland. Hence the decline of the herring fishing hit them hardest of all. Today, Stornoway District is handicapped geographically, by distance from the markets; historically, by its late entry into the industry; and economically, in that it failed to participate in the trend towards the centralisation of the industry in share-holding companies within easy reach of London.

In the old days of sail it was easy for men to combine the two occupations of crofting and fishing. When in the early years of this century power replaced sail (the first motor fishing boats went to work in 1907) and the steam drifter took over from the sailboat, the whole nature of the fishing industry changed. Modern boats and gear had to be acquired if the work was to be profitable. But the islesmen, partly because of lack of capital, partly because of the lack of suitable anchorages and harbours, and partly because the combination of crofting and fishing had created a seasonal tradition incompatible with the use of expensive boats (which needed to be kept continually at sea if they were to pay at all), were unable to adjust themselves to meet the new challenges. In the inter-war years they had no option but to carry on as best they could in their old traditional role. The resultant decline meant that when opportunities did arise for fishermen generally in the form of grants and loan schemes (introduced in 1945 by the Fisheries Division of the Scottish Home Department and subsequently by the White Fish Authority and the Herring Industry Board), the bulk of the men living in the isles were unable to take advantage of them: they lacked the necessary qualifying experience in handling modern boats and equipment, as well as confidence in fishing as a full-time occupation. By 1959 there were only twenty-five boats of 40 ft or more in length based on Hebridean ports. Lewis had only six full-time crews; Harris had five.

105

This lack of a local fleet fishing in the Minch and associated waters on a full-time basis has inevitably brought reluctance on the part of Government bodies to invest capital in, say, harbour improvements, knowing that they would fail to yield an eventual return. Just after the first world war Lord Leverhulme formulated ambitious plans for a full-time fishing fleet based on Stornoway. More than thirty years later, in 1954, the Taylor Commission, set up to investigate the problems of crofting, summed up:

> Gone are the days when the crew of the fishing boat could haul up their craft on the beach and leave it there in safety. The modern seine-netter is much too heavy to be beached in that way and far too costly to be exposed to risk in unsafe anchorages . . . The capital outlay required for their purchase is such that it is not possible to operate them except on a full-time basis. It is still possible for smaller boats to be employed in fishing for lobster or crab, but the general trend of development is against the man who combines fishing with the work of the croft. We do not think it possible to reverse this trend; it should be accepted and an attempt made to establish a full-time fishing industry in Western waters.

The first vital step to do just this was taken in January 1959 when the MacAulay (Rhodesia) Trust announced the introduction of a scheme to 'increase the number of modern boats with efficient crews operating from or based on Lewis'. This Trust was set up under the will of the late Murdo MacAulay of Ness, who left Lewis with little English, less money, but plenty of Gaelic and enterprising spirit, to acquire a considerable fortune in Rhodesia. He bequeathed the bulk of it to be applied for the good of his island home. Anyone applying for assistance under the scheme was required to give an undertaking that he would prosecute fishing on a full-time basis; further, no one would be assisted unless, in the opinion of the trustees, he was likely to make 'an energetic and successful fisherman'. This pioneering venture directly assisted three young men in Kirkibost, Bernera, to acquire one of the best-equipped lobster boats in Scotland; and secondly it acted as a useful prototype for the Government scheme which was to augment and largely replace it a year later. In January 1960 the Government officially instituted the Outer Hebrides Fisheries Training Scheme. Free training was offered to men pre-

General view of the town of Stornoway. Broad Bay is in the far background; the street on the right is South Beach

Blackface sheep: a typical Lewis scene and an essential element in the island's economy

pared to make fishing their career, together with financial assistance to those who satisfactorily completed their training and who wished to acquire boats of their own. This Scheme is now run by the Highlands & Islands Development Board. The Board's participation in the expansion of the fishing potential around the island has been first-class, with commensurate results from an investment of some £500,000.

Illegal fishing

Like goldfields, the seas around the island have always attracted the unscrupulous, those for whom the word 'conservation' has no meaning, and who are careless of the dangers of over-fishing. Illegal trawling began around the year 1894 and by now has drastically impoverished the inshore fishings to which the Harris and Lewis crofters once looked for a supplement to diet and income. The rapid adoption of efficient trawlers was attended by an increasing number of reports of their poaching within the three-mile territorial limit. Though the islanders tried many times to involve the Government's cruisers for the protection of their shores, the poaching went on, and still continues today. Even some of the violence which attended the early attempts to clear the scum from the sea, as it were, continues, part and parcel of the island's sea-life.

Fish processing

A former freezing plant in Stornoway, run by the Herring Industry Board has been converted into a fish-processing factory. This facility, of great value to the port, is run by Rolf Olsen A/S, a long-established Norwegian company with a successful background in fish processing. The company has received investment aid from the Highlands & Islands Development Board, the Highland Fund and the Stornoway Trust; the latter's interest is significant in that it is the first time in which the funds of the Trust have been invested in a private concern, to help retain Stornoway as a successful fishing port.

The most regular shore-side as distinct from maritime industry is the processing of prawns (scampi, or *nephrops norvegicus*). Two firms buy the prawns at the pierhead, shell, cook and freeze them, subsequently despatching them to various dealers in the south. The local trawlers catch white fish and prawns with the same gear, but whereas most of the prawns are landed locally the white fish goes to Gairloch on the mainland for transportation to the Aberdeen market. Attempts have been made to overcome the distance between the island and good-paying markets: in 1966, by collaboration between Stornoway fishermen and the London Fish Merchants' Association, a consignment of 200 boxes of fish was sent direct from Stornoway to Billingsgate, bypassing Aberdeen. The fish was first frozen, then taken by SS *Clansman* to Mallaig railhead and thence to London by rail. It arrived twenty-six hours after leaving Stornoway, in ample time to catch the day's customers. The experiment is to be repeated at intervals. On occasions in the past, shellfish such as lobsters have been flown to Continental markets.

Lobster and crab fishing is an important part-time occupation in the island. In the past it tended to be rendered uneconomic by the heavy losses (sometimes up to 25 per cent) during transit between Stornoway and Billingsgate, but storage-ponds now help retain a reserve for market demands: a lobster-pond at Stockinish in Harris can hold about 25,000 fish, and the pond at Bernera, Loch Roag, can take 30,000. Marketing is done by an agency on behalf of the fishermen, the value per annum being around £50,000 for lobsters caught in the Stornoway Fishery District, and some £40,000 for prawns. The value of white fish is about £30,000 and of herring about £35,000.

6   TRADE AND INDUSTRY

IN the earliest times, the folk of the island of Harris and Lewis were self-supporting; all that they needed for life as it was lived in those days was available at near hand; their existence was self-contained, the economy virtually self-sufficient. By and large, the only commodities often imported were salt, iron, and, to a certain extent, wood. Rents were paid largely in kind: the produce of agriculture, fishing and labour. Surplus produce was directed to southern markets to bring in the odd shilling or two for which there was really very little need in the island. But once money became important in the national economy, it was not long before it was required in the island economy too. By 1790, if not well before, two or three open boats set out each year from Uig to Glasgow, laden with salt beef and dried salt fish. At about this time, too, changes were making their slow appearance in the island way of life and living. Specialists were being required: smiths, tinkers, shipwrights, netmakers, boatbuilders, weavers, tailors and millers. Each of these craftsmen generally held some cornland, either individually or in shares, and also had some rights in the common ground of the township in which he lived.

CROFTER INDUSTRIES

From the pure crofter class there emerged the crofter-craftsmen. In Lochs, for instance, by the turn of the seventeenth century 80 per cent were registered as fishers and netmakers. In the west, in the parish of Barvas, some 70 per cent were also fishers, with kelp-making as a seasonal occupation. In Stornoway parish, where sub-tenants paid 30s to 60s in rent, with twelve days' service, they sold ling to their tacksmen at 5d each, earned 20s a month on herring boats, made kelp at 30s a ton, and worked on roads for 8d per day.

In Harris in 1895, the eight trained male weavers worked for the gentry only. Weaving for the populace was done by the

111

womenfolk, giving a ratio of only one male weaver to fifty-five families. In Lewis, male weavers were more common : one to every twenty-five families. The making of whisky was introduced about the seventeenth century. This was in addition to the old drink of home-brewed beer or ale *(lionn)*, and much of it was made to pay rents; it must have consumed a considerable quantity of valuable foodstuff. However, the spread of distillation as a legitimate home industry by which the rent could be paid, in kind or by sale, was followed by legislation prohibiting all but very large stills; illegal distilling of course went on in a small way.

It was, then, by a very narrow margin that subsistence was won in the island some two centuries ago. Many times famine showed how close was the wolf to the island doors. The introduction of the potato, and the interest in the fishing industry led to an increase in the population, though as discussed in Chapter 3 this in turn brought more problems. Basically, the island economy had never been organised on a sound foundation, with the result that winds of change blew where they would with little or no control.

A new factor in the island economy was introduced after 1750. This was kelp-making, the cutting and burning of seaweed on the shore for subsequent use in the manufacture of alkali for the glass and soap industries. The first tentative move in the island was made by MacLeod of Harris in 1748, when he allowed some Irish labourers to make kelp on his shores; so little was the product's value realised at the time that he only charged them 2s per ton manufactured. As the burning of kelp came to be understood, and the marketable value of the product ascertained, the native population set to. Between 1772 and 1864, about 50 tons were produced in Lewis each year, compared with some 800 tons per annum in the Uists; the Harris figure was 500-600 tons. The growth of the industry began to snowball, and the Minister of Lochs, writing in the *Old Statistical Account*, states that at the time (1796) some 50 tons were being produced in that parish per annum. In Stornoway parish, though no figure is available, the minister reports that kelp-burning was the principal manufacture, and that everyone able to fill a creel, or carry one, was employed at it for about three months of the year. Little of it seems to have been done in Barvas parish. The price of kelp varied according to the amount of barilla (its great competitor, a carbonate of soda made from plant ashes) which found its way into the British market. When the American war interfered with the imports the kelp price was as high as £22 per ton. Prices began to decline about 1810, and from 1822 successive reductions in duties on salt and barilla resulted in the decline and demise of the kelp industry. As a consequence great distress appeared in those districts which had founded their whole economy on seaweed.

The weeds of most value to the industry, because they yielded most salts, included *laminaria digitata, laminaria bulbosa, ascophyllum nodosum* and *fucus serratus*. One ton of kelp yielded an average of 8 lb of iodine, with certain quantities of chloride of sodium, chloride of potassium, and carbonate of soda. When subjected to special treatment and distillation, 2-3 cwts of sulphate of ammonia, and several gallons of naphtha, paraffin oil, and volatile oil were also derived.

The fishing industry, discussed in the previous chapter, took over where the kelp-making industry left off and became another king-pin in the island economy. By the end of the last century it seemed set fair for continuing prosperity. In 1900, harbours were being planned and built with State aid in Uig, at Carloway, Ness and Tarbert. Then 1914 came, and with it sweeping changes in international trade. Island fishermen were left workless with wrecked and rotting fishing boats. In twenty years the number of Scotland's fishermen was halved; the remainder were all but ruined. The islanders' fate mirrored this pattern.

Yet another significant source of income for island families for almost 200 years came from the men in military service, who either sent money home or returned home with their gratuities and pay. In the wars of the last century many enlisted in the Highland regiments, the Navy and the Merchant Marine. Even today, the income from this external activity is not insignificant.

EIGHTEENTH-CENTURY ECONOMY

Information and statistics about the economy of the island in the middle of the eighteenth century are to be found in Walker's *Economical History of the Hebrides or Western Islands of Scot-*

land; his MS is in the British Museum. Lewis is described as being let by Mr MacKenzie of Seaforth for £1,200, which works out at about ½d per acre. The following list of prices of commodities indicates the main produce of the island:

The best driving cows at a medium each	£1	6	0
The Lewes stone of butter (23lb English) per stone	0	7	0
The stone of cheese	0	2	6
The stone of washed wool	0	9	0
The grass of a cow for a whole summer	0	1	8
Kelp, per ton	3	5	0
Aqua Vitae, per Anchor (26 Scotch pints)	1	5	0
Dog-fish oil (per barrel)	2	5	0
Herrings, per barrel	1	2	0
Salmon, per barrel	1	16	0
Dried ling, per hundred	3	15	0

The exports were listed as follows:

700 black cattle; about 100 are sold to ye shipping that put in at Stornoway, and 300 are sent, salted, to ports on the Clyde. The value of the whole is about	£1,430	0	0
Last year about 150 ton of kelp was made and exported	162	5	0
There are twelve stills in Lewes and from these was exported 200 Anchors of Aqua Vitae	250	0	0
Dog-fish oil, 140 barrels	315	0	0
Dried ling, 17,000	637	10	0
Herrings, 750 barrels	1,575	0	0
Salmon, 48 barrels	86	0	0
The spinning school at Stornoway from October 1763 to December 1764 produced 2,288 spindles of linen yarn	228	16	0

Also exported were dried cod, mud cod, above 2,000 sheep skins with wool on them, and some 38 stones of feathers. 'The Lewes neither imports nor exports grain', but mackerel was also an item of export: 'The fishers on the west coast of the island cure a great deal, which are barrelled and sent to the West Indies. The only article of woolen manufacture that the people of Lewes pursue is some coarse blanketing which they send to the Clyde, but their negligence even in ye article appears from their sending out annual above 2000 of wool out of the country unmanufacture.'

Harris was rented at £600. Exports were some 100 tons of kelp (£325), and the value of 250 black cattle exported alive, with 100 salted, was £445. Small quantities of cheese, wool, and the skins of sheep, otters and seals were exported. Grain was neither imported nor exported.

> The plough, which is used here, and in most places of the long island, is of a very peculiar construction. Its length is but 4 feet 7 inches, and is drawn by four horses abreast. It has but one handle by which it is directed; the mold board is fastened with two leather thongs, and the soke and coulter are bound together at the point by a rim of iron. Beside kelp, there is little else manufactured, except a little coarse woolen yarn, and some blanketing, which they send yearly to Glasgow. They raise a little flax of which they make some coarse linen for their own use, but import all the fine linen which they consume. In the year 1756, an American vessel in distress was obliged to put out three hogsheads of lintseed in Harris, which was sown and afforded crops of lint which were above double the value of the usual crops. The east and west of Loch Tarbert in the Harris are every year revisited by the herring shoals. During the five years from 1743 to 1747, the west loch was the principal seat of the herring fishery. About thirty vessels from 18 to 40 tons, belonging to Campbelltown, Greenock, and Irvine, were completely loaded each of these years at this place.

With even a modest amount of business taking place, it was a natural step to establish commercial facilities. Stornoway men who once acted as agents became shopkeepers. The increase in the use of money attracted banks. During the Seaforth ownership of Lewis, the island had its own currency or notes, designed and printed from plates in the same style as the modern banknote. The wording ran: 'I promise to pay on demand to the Chamberlain of the Lewis or Bearer ONE POUND Sterling at the Counting Room here.' The notes carried a date and were signed by the proprietor, J. A. Stewart MacKenzie. It is not known for certain how long the notes remained in currency, when they ceased to be used, or even whether they were officially acceptable. At one time, as rare items, they fetched high prices from collectors. A number were found in a warehouse in Leith some years ago; a few found their way back to Stornoway, where one can be seen in the Public Library.

Today, with kelp long forgotten and fishing of minor importance, it is the Harris Tweed industry which supports many of the island people, either directly or indirectly; an island cottage industry with exports earnings exceeding £2,500,000 a year. Harris Tweed is exported to some thirty countries, including America, Canada, Australia, New Zealand, Japan and all the European nations. The industry is in fact the basis of prosperity in the area, both dependent upon and supporting the crofter-weaver working at the handloom in his home. Seven million yards of tweed are woven annually by the independent weavers 'on the books' of the various mills. The weavers must finance themselves, buying their own looms and bobbins, equipping and maintaining their workshops. Though they receive their supplies of yarn from the mills, they are graded as self-employed persons and as such are not entitled to unemployment benefit—a subject which has caused much argument.

One of the most outstanding facts about the cloth is that its essential qualities have remained unchanged since the industry's early formative years. But it has astonishing versatility and over 5,000 patterns are available, including the crotal browns and the heather colours.

A weaver on average can produce about $2\frac{1}{2}$ webs, or tweeds, each week, a web measuring about 80 yd by $28\frac{1}{2}$ in, and gets a reward of some £8 per web, according to the intricacies of the design or the number of colours involved. The money is paid out by a mobile bank making the rounds of the townships throughout the island. It is reckoned that the mills, for their part, make 1d to 6d a yard profit, depending on turnover; the total annual value of the industry's output is in the region of £4,000,000.

Between them, the five mills in Stornoway and the one in Shawbost consume two-thirds of the Scottish wool clip—the native Western Islands' crop is sufficient for less than a month's production. A thousand pounds of raw wool end up as 885 yards of finished cloth. About 1,000 workers are employed at the mills, representing about 95 per cent of the island's industry—not counting, of course, the 1,200 or so self-employed weavers. The Shawbost mill, started in 1915 in a very small way, employs about seventy people from the surrounding crofting community on dyeing the wool, carding it and spinning it into yarn, and has about 500 weavers on its books. In 1955 it became a limited company and a £35,000 finishing plant was added; other recent extensions have been made to the tune of £70,000. The establishment of such a large industrial complex in one of the remotest parts of Britain is an achievement to be underlined.

The early cloth industry

Coarse woollen cloth has been made in the Hebrides, as in other rural Highland areas, from time immemorial. Rents were often paid in blankets or plaiding. In 1656, 'pladding' was one of the items of trade brought by Highland boats to Glasgow for sale there. In the late eighteenth century, blackfaced sheep were introduced into the Highlands and islands; the fleece from this breed was much heavier than that of the native sheep and consequently proved ideal raw material for local woollen manufacture for trade. In the Hebrides, the product was mainly for domestic and local consumption. The people of Harris, however, were well known for the excellence of their weaving which found a limited external market. In 1844, the Earl of Dunmore, the first non-native proprietor of Harris, had the Murray tartan copied in tweed by local weavers, so successfully that the Earl and his enterprising wife encouraged improvements in the product and introduced it to their friends. The cloth, ideal for outdoor pursuits such as fishing and stalking, found ready wearers. In 1857, an Edinburgh lady went about getting orders for the Harris weavers, and business increased so much that in 1888 she moved to London and opened a small depot for tweeds.

Thus by the time the nineteenth century had reached maturity tweed was becoming well known, and weavers and local merchants, usually shopkeepers, developed sales contacts on the mainland. At that time every web of tweed produced was unique: it could never be copied exactly. This of course added to its charm in the eyes of the more sophisticated purchasers, as did the domestic and primitive conditions of its manufacture. All processes were carried out by hand. The wool was washed and dyed out of doors beside any convenient stream where a big black pot could be set up on stones and heated by firing peats. Carding, a tedious and unpleasant task, spinning and weaving were done in the 'black houses' of the crofters, which often lacked chimneys or proper windows: the tweed acquired more by accident than design a definite 'peat reek', which was duly considered to be another of its attractions, combining with the mainland town-dwellers' pleasant thoughts of Hebridean thatched cottages, peat fires and natural dyes from island moors and shores, to give the cloth something of a romantic aura.

Development

The increased demand brought problems however. Carding by hand was a slow business and quite unable to keep up with the weavers' requirements for raw material, so wool was sent to mainland mills for carding. But this introduced an element of suspicion, for the product was not now wholly Hebridean. To get round this, Sir Samuel Scott, the proprietor of Harris in 1900, opened a water-powered carding mill at Tarbert, Harris. In 1903, this example was followed up by a Stornoway merchant, Aeneas MacKenzie, who started a carding mill near the Patent Slip (one of Matheson's enterprises) in Stornoway. Non-profitmaking bodies (the Scottish Home Industries Association and the Crofters' Agency) began to open up more depots for the receipt of tweeds. In addition to the original depots at Stornoway and Tarbert, others were established at Obbe (now Leverburgh), Uig in Lewis, and in North and South Uist.

The Congested Districts Board also took an interest, appointing a travelling instructor who was responsible for the introduction of better cloth designs and other improvements including the flying shuttle. This latter was a distinct advantage over the old method used on the 'beart bheag' (the traditional small wooden loom), where the shuttle was a sheep's shin bone thrown by hand. The board also paid grants for the improvement of looms, and large black pots were sent to Uig to enable the people there to dye larger batches of wool to maintain uniformity of colour through the whole web.

Lewis tweed

Suddenly Lewis came on the Harris Tweed scene. It had been slow to enter the industry; most of its employment was on works related to public boards and on the private constructions of the Matheson regime. Fishing, too, yielded a reasonable living to most of the Lewis crofters, so the incentive to weave had been small. But about 1880, following the death of Sir James Matheson, expenditure on the Matheson property was severely curtailed; and also about this time fish sales by auction replaced private contracts between fishermen and curers, making fishing far less remunerative to those crofters who had worked as hired hands. So Lewis took to cloth making, taking advantage of the increased demand, which could no longer be met ·by the Harris workers. Records of tweed production are few until after 1880, but whereas in 1899 there were only 55 looms in Lewis, as reported to the Congested Districts Board, in 1906 this had increased to 161, and by 1911 there were some 300. There was some initiative in London too : in 1906 a person was convicted for selling as 'Harris Tweed' a cloth woven on a power loom.

As the number of island weavers increased, so did the demand for yarn even further outpace the capacity of the domestic spinning wheels. Cheap, mill-spun yarn was imported and this, added to inferior weaving, gave rise to the name 'Stornoway Tweed', indicating a poor-quality cloth. In 1907 the Scottish Home Industries Association closed its Stornoway depot because the amount of hand-spun yarn used did not justify its continued existence. The Crofters Agency, however, kept open its depots at Balallan and Uig. Around this time, therefore, two products were on the market with the same name : a 100 per cent true hand-spun tweed, and a tweed made wholly or partly of mill-spun yarn. In Stornoway it was appreciated that the use of mill-spun yarn did not necessarily result in a poor-quality cloth, and this initiated some new moves. Spinning machinery was added to the Patent Slip carding mill, and in 1906 Kenneth MacKenzie began a new carding and spinning mill.

Thus were laid the lines of a new form of economic organisation for Lewis. At first, tweed manufacture here, as in Harris, was strictly a domestic activity: the wool of the crofter's own sheep was clipped, washed and dyed, carded, spun at home, and woven into cloth by persons in the township with the skill to produce a suitable cloth; the weaving was a part-time and mainly female occupation. Payment for the weaving was in kind: peats, potatoes, or labour. The waulking or finishing of the cloth was mostly a communal activity carried out by the womenfolk, who turned it into a particular social occasion with definite feminine characteristics. If the cloth made was in excess of domestic requirements, the crofter sold it directly to a customer, or else the local shopkeeper bought it or gave credit for it.

With the rise in weaving for a definite market in Lewis, all this changed. Weaving became a full-time specialist occupation and, partly because the flying shuttle made the work heavier, it became predominantly male work. With the use of mill-spun yarn there grew up a number of merchants, the Lewis 'producers', who bought yarn either locally or from the mainland, and put it out for weaving and hand finishing on a commission basis. The yarn and the resulting cloth remained their property. At times the cloth embodied a handspun weft; at other times perhaps no handspun was used at all. As pointed out above, it was marketed as Harris Tweed, as was the 100 per cent handspun cloth, yet it cost about 21d to produce compared with 36d for the 'real' tweed. The cheaper type provided Lewis's rapidly-expanding output between 1900 and 1911, and by that year Lewis had outstripped Harris. In 1912, the handspun yardage produced in Harris was 175,000; partially and wholly millspun accounted for some 4,000 yards; and the total value was £26,500. In Lewis the yardage of handspun cloth was some 10,000; but about 340,000 yards of partially or wholly millspun was sold. The total Lewis value was £44,000.

The trade mark

When eventually the question arose of some mark to distinguish between the two cloths, it was with difficulty that the Harris merchants persuaded the Board of Trade that a distinction was necessary. In the end, an application was made in 1909 to that body for a trade mark defining Harris Tweed as 'tweed, hand-spun, hand-woven and dyed and finished by hand in the Outer Hebrides', with 'made in Harris' or 'made in Lewis' added as appropriate. The Harris merchants had to join forces with their former rivals in the tweed-marketing business, the voluntary non-profit-making Associations. To inspect the cloth and stamp it with a trade mark—an orb surmounted by a cross—a Harris Tweed Association was formed, consisting of representatives of each of the Harris merchants, the Crofters Agency and the Scottish Home Industries Association. Cloth was first stamped in 1911. In 1912, some Stornoway merchants were granted representation in the Harris Tweed Association, which still exists for the benefit of the industry.

In 1934, the definition of 'Harris Tweed' was eased to include any cloth 'made from pure virgin wool, produced in Scotland, spun, dyed and finished in the Outer Hebrides and hand-woven by the Islanders at their own homes in the islands of Lewis, Harris, Uist, Barra and their several purtenances and all known as the Outer Hebrides'. It was further provided that 'Woven in Harris', 'Woven in Lewis', etc, could be added, and also 'Handspun' in the case of tweeds made entirely from hand-spun yarns.

Today, a few Harris families maintain the old tradition, hand-dyeing and carding, spinning on the wheel, hand-weaving and finishing, producing a high-quality article mainly for individual customers. These tweeds rightly command up to three times the price for the general run of tweed.

OTHER INDUSTRIES

It was not until the era of Sir James Matheson that anything like a truly industrial activity was attempted. Matheson, a native of Shinness in the parish of Lairg, Sutherland, was born in 1796. Aged seventeen, he decided on a commercial career and took himself to London. After two years in a mercantile house, he went to Calcutta, where he worked in the counting-house of MacKintosh

& Co. The call of the Far East drew him away from India to Canton, where he set up business as an agent acting for firms in India. During the period 1815-20 he met William Jardine, from Dumfriesshire, who first glimpsed the mainland of China as a surgeon's mate from the deck of an East Indiaman three years before Trafalgar. Jardine left the East India Company in 1817 after sixteen years' service and, having with native prudence accumulated enough capital to set up on his own account, entered into an agreement with an East India merchant of London and a Bombay trader to operate the new ship *Sarah*. In 1832 Matheson and Jardine combined forces and interests to form Jardine, Matheson & Co, 'The Firm', as it has been known ever since those early days of commerce in the Far East. The unique experience which its founders and their successors have accumulated in providing services for manufacturers, and handling trade with more than a quarter of the world's population, is virtually unparalleled in the annals of British mercantile enterprise.

Matheson amassed a fortune. In 1842 he returned to his native Scotland, and finding that the Lewis estate was up for sale he bought it for £190,000 from the Estate Trustees. The island, at that time a truly isolated backwater, provided him with plenty of scope for ideas and work for deep pockets. He died on the last day of 1878. It has been estimated to the pound sterling that, including the purchase price of Lewis, Matheson spent over £574,363. More than £100,000 was spent in erecting Lews Castle and in laying out the grounds, which work provided his impoverished tenants with a means to earn something with which to buy their necessities. Briefly, Matheson drained land and reclaimed it; he planted trees; he built roads, bridges and quays; he excited anew an interest in the fishing industry and built premises for fish curing; he built a patent boat-slip for the contruction and repair of fishing and other craft; he established schools and paid the teachers' salaries; he also built a brick-works and a chemical works to distil paraffin from peat. He is remembered in Stornoway's Matheson Road : little else remains of his extensive efforts.

The Lewis Chemical Works

But it must at least be recorded that he made the first-ever attempts at introducing a true industrial activity on a large scale : the Lewis Chemical Works, which cost him some £33,000. The basis of the enterprise was the real possibility of turning the Lewis peat bogs into oil. The idea was sound enough, but incompetent management killed it off; its death was hastened with the discovery of natural oils in America and in the Middle East.

An experimental plant was built near Lews Castle. Another was erected on the banks of the River Creed, and to protect the salmon for which this river is famous, Matheson had to spend considerable sums in trying to keep the discharge effluent out of the waters. A third distillation plant was erected, this time well away from the Castle grounds. A kiln was built, elaborate condensers were fitted up, peat was cut and stacked, and a canal, three-quarters of a mile long, was cut to convey the peat to the plant. Troubles were considerable, despite the efforts of a chemist brought by Matheson from London. In time, the plant began to produce. Each working day of twenty-four hours, about 18 tons of peat were used in the kilns; another $3\frac{1}{2}$ tons were used to fire the boilers. The recovery figure of crude hydrocarbons was around 5 per cent.

With reasonable success in sight, work was put in hand for the building of tramways across the peat bogs so that the material could be obtained from a greater area. Also, a refining plant was built at Garrabost, eight miles away from the distilling plant, which added greatly to costs and increased the inconvenience so far as managing the plant was concerned. For some ten years, the Lewis Chemical Works produced quite valuable products. One of the first, which found a good market, was a lubricant for wagon axles and heavy machinery; within a short time of its introduction the demand exceeded the supply. But, instead of increasing production, the management authorised the addition of water to a 3-ton consignment for Glasgow to fulfill a rush order. It came back by the next steamer; and further orders for it dwindled to nothing.

It was a ship's captain who discovered that the peat tar was an excellent anti-fouling grease for ships' bottoms. Samples were sent to several shipping ports, and the response was good; one Liverpool chandler even offered to take the whole output at a good price. But again the product was rendered useless, this time by being subjected to a partial-distillation process, in the thought that this would improve it; orders stopped. One shale-oil firm offered to take the crude peat tar to refine along with its own products for the purpose of modifying the flash-point of the oil it was itself manufacturing. Most commercial enterprises would have jumped at the chance of disposing of their output without the need for the always-tricky refining process, but here personal interests intervened and another avenue of profit was blocked.

The Lewis Chemical Works had by this time become something of a showpiece, chemists and scientists mecca-ing their way to Stornoway to see both plant and product. One eminent chemist pronounced the plant one of the most successful ever erected for the distillation of hydrocarbon oils from peat, and an Irishman said that if the Irish Peat Company's installation had been as successful as the Lewis counterpart, Ireland would have been enriched by her peat bogs. By the middle of the 1860s a ton of peat tar was being produced for 70s, as against 100s for unrefined shale oil. Peat oil sold at first at 2s 9d per gallon, then dropped to 2s 6d and finally to 2s, presumably as the American oil products were reaching the market. The writing was on the wall. Sir James Matheson, realising too late that perhaps a closer control should have been applied to the venture from the beginning, decided to cut his losses and close the works. All the metal—condensers, pumps, stills, pipes, and tanks—was broken up and sold for scrap. Nearly four miles of light railway had been laid from the Creed Works to the peat bogs; this was lifted for scrap. So ended the first phase of industrial Lewis. The venture proved, however, that with adequate skill and knowledge success could be grasped.

Bricks, printing, whisky

The brickworks which Matheson built for £6,000 at Garrabost produced building materials and some fine examples of draining tiles, but has now disappeared. The Patent Slip built at Stornoway for another £6,000 was able to take ships of up to

124

(*above*) Weaving Harris Tweed in a crofter's home; it is usually done in a byre or shed on the croft. View taken from the warp end of the loom

(*below*) Setting up the loom

(*above*) An island industry, small but socially significant: the seaweed processing factory at Keose, Loch Erisort, Lewis

(*below*) Feeding wet seaweed into the factory's drying plant. The dried product is milled and exported by puffer for subsequent processing

800 tons and had a steam-driven winch. The slip has also vanished—except for the name of the Patent Slip Wool Mills, which produce Harris Tweed.

Other small industrial activities in the island during the nineteenth century included the business of Alexander MacPherson, chemist, druggist, stationer and printer, who set up in Stornoway in 1842. He brought across the Minch with him Lewis's first demy-size hand printing press, which was still in use on 1 January 1889 to produce the first issue of the short-lived *The Lewisman*. Copies of this earliest Lewis newspaper can be seen at Stornoway Public Library. Early in the 1890s Thomas Nicolson also set up as a printer.

Whisky was once an important product, not only for local consumption, but also for export. One of the Privy Council's main indictments against the islanders in the Hebrides in 1622 was that they seized any cargo of wine and spent 'bothe dayis and nightis in thair excesse of drinking'. The council therefore enacted that masters of vessels sailing Hebridean waters should carry no more wines. It has been suggested that this and other measures were responsible for the beginning of illicit distilling, which in Lewis continued overtly as late as 1827. One of the two principal stills established by Lord Seaforth in the island at that time was at Coll, a few miles from Stornoway, the other at Gress, a few miles farther on. Such was the fame of these stills, both for output and quality, that it was hard to choose between 'Coll' or 'Gress'. Sometimes, the product passed as an article of exchange in the island, and the factor received a considerable part of the rents in it instead of money; but the stills were closed about 1870. The *Inverness Courier* of 14 November 1827 remarks virtuously: 'Owing to the vigilance of Captain Oliver, of the Revenue cutter "Prince of Wales", and the new Excise Officers on shore, smuggling is so completely put down in the Long Island that there is actually not a drop of illicit whisky to be got from the Butt of Lewis to Barra Head; and there is probably at this moment a larger supply of legal whisky from Greenock for the supply of Stornoway alone, than was ever imported into the Hebrides before.'

TRADE AND INDUSTRY

Lord Leverhulme's fisheries

The era of Lord Leverhulme, the soap magnate, is well documented; a complicated story and not yet told in full. The confrontation of a dynamic industrialist from England with the deep-thinking crofter of Lewis has formed the subject of much speculation, particularly with regard to the non-success—rather than failure—of Leverhulme's schemes for the island. Leverhulme bought Lewis in 1918. He had visited the island about twenty years before and had no doubt thought that with proper direction and adequate capital much could be done to bring it out into a fresh, lively economic air, profitable both to himself and the inhabitants. He was a visionary; but he was also a practical man, with great successes in the commercial world to prove it. In 1919, contracts were placed with Sir Robert MacAlpine Limited to begin operations in Stornoway : excavating, levelling and building in preparation for the new town and its factories. The Leverhulme Syndicate bought deep-sea trawlers in Aberdeen, Hull, Fleetwood and other ports, and also retail fish shops in many towns on the mainland. This side of the enterprise was known as The Mac Fisheries Limited, and the island developments were under the direction of the 'Lewis & Harris Welfare & Development Company Limited'.

Leverhulme's main idea was to establish Stornoway as the centre of a great fishing and fish-processing industry. As he put it, acre for acre the seas surrounding the Hebrides were infinitely richer than the land. He maintained that in any programme for the improvement of the islanders' economic position, fishing must become their primary if not their only activity. Such, however, was the land hunger of returning ex-servicemen that his attentions were almost wholly given over to trying to persuade those wanting crofts that they would be, materially at least, better off in his canning factories. But farms were broken up to satisfy the demand for land until the time came when Leverhulme felt he had to abandon Lewis. The Board of Agriculture and the Scottish Office were also principal actors in the play, mostly on the side of the land raiders who squatted on farm land in the island so causing the farms' eventual fragmentation into small units of economic insignificance. When he pulled out of Lewis to go south to Harris, he offered—such was the character of the man—as thanks for the '98 per cent support' he got from the people of Lewis, to each Lewis crofter his own croft as a free gift, and the Lews Castle, together with all his property in Stornoway, to the people of the town.

In 1919, Leverhulme became proprietor of Harris, and concentrated his efforts in Obbe, now called Leverburgh, in South Harris. The harbour at Obbe lacked the natural advantage which Stornoway had, so he spent large sums on making it navigable. Rocky obstacles were blasted away; numerous buoys and beacons were set up to guide vessels into harbour; new quays were built; and kippering sheds, and other buildings necessary for packing and curing herring were erected. Among his other undertakings in Harris were the provision of a mill for making tweeds, and he bore half the cost of the $5\frac{1}{2}$ miles of road between Leverburgh and Finsbay. In 1925, after a visit to the Congo, he died in Brussels. His Harris schemes came to an abrupt end. And the remains of industrial history are still to be seen in the quietness of the little township named after one of the most stormy of business petrels that Britain has ever seen.

Tourism

Tourism has always been a perfunctory and casual affair, until the introduction of the fast ferries which now link the mainland (via Skye) with the Outer Isles. Some 10,000 cars cross each year from Skye to the Hebrides. In 1913, the Stornoway Tourist Association had a struggle to increase the number of visitors to the town, to establish it as a tourist resort. It is much the same today with the Western Isles Tourist Association, which is having difficulty in integrating tourist facilities with crofting activities. In Lewis, the Stornoway Trust has assisted in establishing pony-trekking, a venture which has the potential to mirror the success of a similar one in the Isle of Skye.

PRESENT INDUSTRY

Almost an echo of the kelp-burning industry is the alginate industry. It provides employment for only small numbers, but is a useful crofting ancillary which, unlike many others, is soundly based on a definite commercial demand. Various industries use the extracted acid for some 150 products. The Scottish alginate industry, the second largest in the world, is based on the process of E. C. Stanford, who discovered alginic acid in 1883, though today modern methods are used. For raw materials it has turned to the old kelping shores of the Hebrides and Northern Isles. On the island it has a factory at Keose on Loch Erisort, a site chosen for the easy access afforded to puffers; the factory receives the weed, dries, mills and bags it, and the boats then carry 200-ton loads to Girvan. The factory itself involved some £30,000 of capital layout and has a capacity of 120 wet tons per week—4 wet tons producing 1 dry milled ton. About a dozen Harris and Lewis crofters gather the seaweed crop, the most useful type being bladderwrack or rockweed *(ascophyllum nodosum)*, from the shores at Loch Erisort, East Loch Roag and Bernera in Lewis, Husinish and Scarp in Harris, and Loch Seaforth. Where there is road access the weed is cut by sickle and loaded into a lorry, but more often it is cut at low water to be floated with the incoming tide and rafted to Keose, hauled by motor boat.

A product of the land not readily associated with the Hebrides is bulbs. Bulb-growing deserves a mention, however, if only because the experiment to see whether it could become a commercial possibility in Lewis was carried out by the children of Lionel (Ness) Junior Secondary School. The MacAulay (Rhodesia) Trust made an investment of £150 to cover initial expenses, and success followed. When the original project was completed it was extended, sales bringing the school a useful sum. But an attack of disease brought production to a standstill in 1966.

Another small industry is the aerated-water plant at Ness, which is operating with reasonable success, and could do better if imports of aerated waters from abroad were reduced. A number of recent surveys made in the island have found great interest in such activities as shell-fish processing in Harris to produce semi-preserves, using mostly cockles and mussels. Local knitting already has a name for its products and a potential for extension on a commercial scale; this latter began in late 1966. Some forty years ago knitting specialists went to Lewis to investigate the possibilities

130

of a knitting industry based on the crofters, who would use Lewis yarn and produce knitwear in addition to their woven fabrics. However, it was found that the yarns used for Harris Tweed were unsuitable for knitwear, not being given sufficient twist in the spinning: before women use this tweed yarn for knitting, it is common practice to twist two or more threads of yarn together on a hand spinning-wheel.

Little in the way of craft work is done on the island, mainly because of the lack of indigenous materials which could be used to produce typically-island items. Marram-grass has been suggested as being suitable for making agricultural wind-breaks, and close-woven basket-work. Shore-stones and pebbles are plentiful both in quantity and variety of type and colour.

Small employment outlets on the island are marine and motor engineering, mainly based on Stornoway, and boat-building. This latter is a small but socially-significant firm in Ness with products with a high reputation. Construction and general building is of some significance, one of the most enterprising firms being built up literally from scratch so as to become a highly-successful island business.

The unemployment problem

The island's unemployment problem is as much a matter of concern today as it has ever been, averaging about 25 per cent annually (representing well over 1,000 people) compared with the Scottish mainland figure of 6.0 per cent; the contemporary figure for Britain is around 3.0 per cent. While unemployment as it affects adults is serious enough, unemployment among teenagers threatens the community's whole future. The island has its Youth Employment Officer, who has an unenviable task. Each junior and secondary school in the island is visited to interview school-leavers, at least once a year; employment advice is given and this is supplemented by Careers Officers' visits.

Such employment openings as exist over the island's limited spectrum are concentrated in Stornoway. They are, however, mainly in shop work, mill work and hotel work for girls, with a few vacancies for apprentices in trades generally associated with building construction. Most of the jobs offered are very much in

131

the nature of stopgaps in the younger, formative years and do not offer progressive training for the eventual chosen career. As an example of this, a number of island girls come to Stornoway to work in local shops and then leave the island after two years or so to take up hotel work or nursing on the mainland; many boys leave the island for apprenticeship training in trades which now require evening-class, day- or block-release educational classes. About fifty young persons leave the island each year under the Training Allowances Scheme of the Youth Employment Service, which financially assists them to live in lodgings while working away from home.

Most of the employment categories in the island of course employ less than a handful of people, either full-time adults or time-serving apprentices; they are fully staffed very quickly and opportunities arise only when an employee dies or leaves the island, or—more rarely—when an increased demand for a service (for instance television engineering at one time) creates vacancies for apprentices.

7   THE PEOPLE

THOUGH there are a number of large island communities in the British Isles, Harris and Lewis have in particular retained their individual characteristics, mainly because the Minch has acted as a buffer against effective infiltration of alien influences. The relative insularity of the north-west Highlands has enhanced this isolation, to preserve what is probably one of the oldest forms of communal life in Britain. It has some unique characteristics which are evident even in these days of sophisticated civilisation. The basis of life, although today the individual is beginning to show face, is a communal spirit, based on team-work. Work undertaken with the willing help of others is easier, lighter and quicker done: livestock is easier handled in a large controlled flock; boats are best rowed with a crew. And the women, with the same inborn communal spirit, once spun yarn together; waulked or fulled the cloth together; and helped each other in childbirth, child-care and the deaths which affected the community.

Several of these teams eventually merged to form what is now called the crofting township. And, though a township may nowadays number 1,000 people, to keep, if not pull, together is still a priority if the social structure is not to fail. Townships have been called in the past, by understanding writers, 'sociable hamlets' and 'little commonwealths'. Though these are of long standing historically, they are still a dynamic form of social integration of the kind found elsewhere only in working-class districts of cities such as Glasgow and Manchester. This is not to say that one must be 'poor' in order to participate in such a society. In the material world, to be poor is to be without money; in a crofting society, lack of money, although this commodity has tended in recent years to assume for itself an out-of-proportion standing and status, does not necessarily mean destitution; for help to keep the body together is always to hand, though the donor may never be seen or known.

THE PEOPLE

Most of the outward changes which have occurred in the island took place in the two decades just after the first world war. Food, for instance, now tends to be better balanced and contains more nutrients. Staple diets in the past were mostly confined to a few items, and based on the potato. Fish, particularly those with essential oils (eg cod) were, of course, available; but only if the fishermen were lucky in the catch. As for vegetables and fresh fruit, it was not until after the 1920s that these became generally available all the year round.

Another outward change has been in dress. Until the beginning of the twenties, the women wore a black petticoat striped with colours, a dark blouse, often with stays, and a knitted muffler round the neck and over the head. In summer, the tartan shawl was more typical of Sunday-wear than of weekdays. Men's clothes tended to be of the homespun type, rich in water-resisting oil. Later these were replaced, so far as the fishermen were concerned, with oilskins, waterproofs and rubber boots. Dress nowadays of course tends to conform to what is displayed in magazines, on the film screen and on television.

The changes in the mental characteristics of a people are not so obvious. Centuries of generations of long-dead forbears have contributed their accretions to the character of the island people today. It is a complex one. Impressions of the island people as such are few, mainly because observers looked for those economic aspects which gave the society its *raison d'être*. That islandfolk of former times were fond of music and dancing was the observation of the Rev John Lane Buchanan, who was 'Missionary Minister to the Isles from the Church of Scotland' from 1782 to 1790. In a volume published in 1793, in which he describes his Hebridean experiences, he says that the British laws had been introduced to the Island of Lewis by the Seaforth of that period. The Lewis people, he says, 'since their late happy change from servitude to freedom, by the present noble-minded proprietor, are animated with such life as to meet in companies, regularly each week, at stated places, where both old and young take their turn in this agreeable past-time [dancing], when they exercise themselves with amazing alertness and spirit.' Martin Martin mentions that in his time (c 1695) the Lewis people were 'very dextrous in the exercises of swimming, archery, vaulting, or leaping'. He also says that they were great lovers of music, and that when he was in the island he heard of eighteen men who could play the violin well without having been taught.

The Rev William MacRae, minister of Barvas, writing in the *New Statistical Account*, gives a description of his parishioners (in 1836) which can be applied to all the country districts in the island at that time. After stating that in their habits much cleanliness can scarcely be expected, considering their poverty and the wretchedness of their habitations, he says :

> Their mode of living most closely approaches the pastoral : without arts, trade, manufacture, navigation, or literature, their whole round of duty consists in securing fuel, in sowing and reaping their scanty crops, and in rearing their flocks, and tending them at pasture. Yet in these limited circumstances, while supplied with food and clothing of the plainest description, and able to pay their rents, their simple cottages are abodes of happiness and contentment. Blue kelt [a thick cloth] is almost the only dress worn by the men, and stuffs, variously striped, by the women, with under dresses of plaiding, all home-made. In many instances, however, cotton shirts and print gowns are beginning to supersede the use of some of these articles . . . Their ordinary food consists of oat and barley meal, potatoes and milk variously prepared. Their domestic economy is frugal and moderate beyond conception. The produce of a foreign soil such as tea, coffee, and sugar, and the common conveniences of art, such as knives, forks, and etc., are to them altogether alien.

It is of interest that the change in dress-types (from woollen homespuns to cotton fabrics) was followed by an increase in the incidence of rheumatism.

Today, the island folk are reputed to be gloomy with a black, depressive attitude towards life. The editor of the *Stornoway Gazette* has pointed out : 'We cannot understand a people and why they act as they do unless we know the content of their memories. We cannot understand the paradox of the naturally gay in heart seeking religious consolation in a grim and gritty Calvinism. We cannot understand why Lewis, which clothes the world in colourful tweeds, clothes most of the women in nothing but black. The young have found the island a much more kindly place. They have never been forced by circumstances to choose between predestination and despair.'

To take account of matters beyond the material level is inherent in the Gaelic Celt. Celtic poetry and song, legend and folklore, all so alive with fancy and so sympathetic towards the things of nature, reflect the inborn sensitivity and character of the present-day Highlander and Islander. Fiction's caricature of the island-dweller (not only in Harris and Lewis, but in the other islands) has been taken by another society with a different cultural background, with insufficient knowledge of historical facts, as being virtually authentic. The Western Isles have had more than their share of 'observers' who have failed to penetrate to the inner Gael. Only with a knowledge of the background, social, cultural, ethnic, historical and so on, can the 'larger than life' islander be seen in perspective—as a normal human being.

RELIGION

There are few communities in the British Isles which have, since the Christian dawning, so closely integrated religious belief with secular day-to-day living as the Harris and Lewis people. Though many times the religious element in island life foundered in a Sargasso Sea of outright superstition, it has managed to survive to its present-day form which might be described as cathartic in nature. When one attempts to investigate religion and superstition as two separate subjects, one is forced to consider either both as one, or one as complementary to the other. Even in those times during the island's history when materialism was prominent, somewhere in the background religion was acknowledged in one form or another.

As mentioned in Chapter 3, in 1610 Lord Kintail brought Farquhar MacRae, the vicar of Gairloch, to Lewis. The first Earl of Seaforth, who built a church in Stornoway (St Lennan's) was nominally Episcopalian. During the temporary supremacy of Episcopacy in Scotland, there was little disturbance in the Highlands of the Presbyterian organisation. The bishops controlled their dioceses; but the ministers controlled their parishioners. In

Lewis, there were but two ministers in 1626, their parishes being Barvas (which included Uig) and Eye, which included Lochs; the population of the island at the time was about 4,000. When Presbyterianism was re-established in Scotland in 1640, the Lewis ministers found no trouble in conforming, as did their fellow parishioners. Sectarian feeling in the island during the seventeenth and eighteenth centuries was not so much between Presbyterians and Episcopalians as between Romanists and Protestants.

In the year 1738, nine Episcopalian Lewismen signed a letter to the Bishop of the Isles, asking for an annual visit from a pastor, being unable to support a full-time minister. Almost a century later in 1839, the foundation stone of St Peter's in Stornoway was laid: this is the town's Episcopal Church. The other building on the island which belongs to the Episcopalians is the ancient church at Eoropie, dating back to the tenth century and perhaps the oldest still in use in the Hebrides; services are held there occasionally, though there is no local Episcopalian congregation. One of the most significant events which echoed right through to the island was the Disruption which took place in Edinburgh in 1843. The result was a 'church spectrum' in Scotland which is still mirrored on a smaller scale in the island: the Church of Scotland, the Free Presbyterian Church, the United Free Church, and the Free Church. The Roman Catholic Church is also represented.

Lewis has one of the largest Free Church congregations in the country. This denomination is particularly known for its outspoken pronouncements from time to time on questions of the day. It is Calvinistic in doctrine and has a reputation for holding the 'Calvinistic outlook' in the more general and pejorative sense; though its strictness may sometimes be over-painted, it is much less liberal in its moral standpoint than is the Church of Scotland, if less austere in some respects than the Free Presbyterians. Its doctrinal position is that of unrelaxed adherence to the Westminster Confession, its ministers and other office-bearers affirming their belief 'in the whole doctrine of the Confession'. It is opposed to theological liberalism and accepts the inerrancy and infallibility of the Scriptures. Only the Psalter is used in public worship, and instrumental music is dispensed with; strong emphasis is laid on evangelical preaching. The Free Church claims 'the free exercise of all its spiritual functions, while it fully admits the State authority in purely temporal concerns'.

Closely tied in with the background of the island folk is the Gaelic language. For many years this has been dying, yet it is still vigorous enough to make a significant contribution to the mental make-up of the people. It is a living language in that it is used for personal communication, though English is often and universally resorted to when the talk turns to technical subjects. As the Gaelic language stands today, by itself it is agreed by most Gaelic speakers to be a barrier to economic progress. The Gaelic-speaking child who also knows English, however, is found to be at no significant disadvantage over the monoglot; indeed, tests have shown, particularly in other multilingual countries, that the bilingual child tends to assimilate knowledge at a greater rate and to a greater depth. Two decades ago a pamphlet issued by the Scottish Council for Research in Education showed that while there were no 'statistically significant' differences between the four areas into which they divided Scotland, the Highlands and Islands came out best in a study of the average level of intelligence:

	Mean	*Standard deviation*
The four Scottish cities	100·86	15·29
The industrial belt	99·19	16·18
The rural areas	100·92	14·52
The Highlands and Islands	101·79	13·13

The pamphlet comments: 'It is interesting that the mean of the most remote and isolated districts is the highest, and the standard of deviation the lowest.'

The Hebrides are now the only area in Scotland where the language, once Scotland's national language, is spoken by a Gaelic-characterised community. On average 95 per cent of the inhabitants of all the island districts are Gaelic-speaking; even in the town of Stornoway, never regarded as wholly Gaelic-speaking, 73 per cent have the language, which has been introduced by immigrant country folk and their descendants.

HEALTH AND HOUSING

Despite the harsh conditions of centuries, the physical health of the island was good in early times. Epidemics were rare due to isolation, though on occasion smallpox carried away many children. The commonest diseases were fevers, jaundice, dysentery and diarrhoea. Bloodletting (as in many another more advanced community) was the usual cure for fevers and dysentery. For coughs the people took a 'brochan' or soup of roots of nettles and reeds boiled in water with yeast; the meal of a black bean, mixed with boiled milk, was a useful cure for dysentery. Reports describe the folk as being well-proportioned, free from bodily imperfections and of good stature; healthful and strong-bodied.

But privations, particularly the frequent recurrences of near-famine, coupled with the primitive housing conditions, began to take their toll. The increasing sickness rate aroused the concern of authority. The most primitive dwellings had but one room, with the cattle at one end and the family at the other. In 1830 Seaforth sought at least to put an end to this, ordering that a partition must be erected between beast and man, 'and that more light should be admitted into the dark recesses of their habitation'. This type of one-room dwelling was not confined to the island, being found with many variants throughout the Highlands and Islands area. The old Lewis house was, as a rule, an oblong structure, varying in length according to the means and requirements of the occupier. It had but one door, and frequently had no windows. Chimneys did not find favour, mainly because any opening for the escape of smoke from the centrally-sited hearth tended to reduce the quality of soot produced; and soot was regarded as a valuable manurial product. If there was a hole in the roof to admit some light, a small pane of glass was fixed into it : this soon had a coating of soot, and the sole source of light was the doorway—when the door was open. The family and the cattle used the same entrance; and the cows' dung was removed once a year in the springtime.

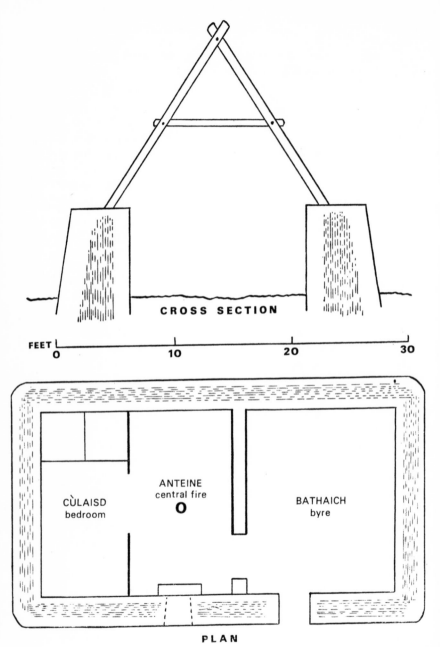

CROSS SECTION

FEET 0   10   20   30

CÙLAISD
bedroom

ANTEINE
central fire
O

BATHAICH
byre

PLAN

Hebridean type of 'black house': plan and cross-section

140

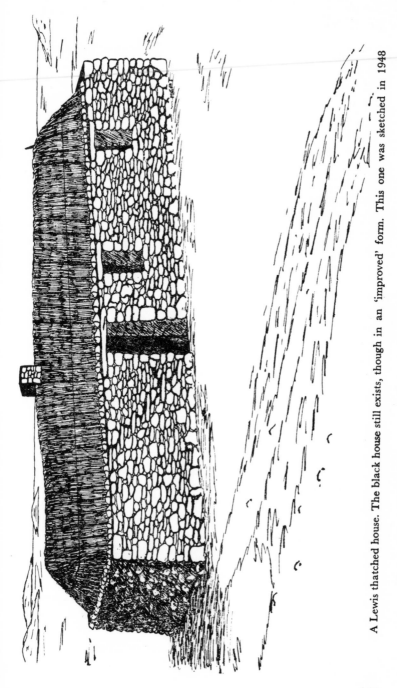

A Lewis thatched house. The black house still exists, though in an 'improved' form. This one was sketched in 1948

141

THE PEOPLE

In 1899, the Medical Officer of Health for the Parish of Barvas described the typical Lewis crofter's house of the time. It had three apartments, two for the family, and a third for the cattle; this new arrangement was the result of the Regulations issued by Sir James Matheson for the betterment of the estate. The low thick walls were built of stone, or stone and turf, with a packing of loose earth, and were perennially damp. The roof, composed of a framework of wooden rafters and couples resting on the inner edge of these walls, was covered over with turf divots and straw, bound with ropes of straw, heather or coarse thatching rope, and weighted down with stones. It was never air- or water-tight, and roof water usually soaked into the packing of the walls and thus oozed into the house. Further, only the slightest attention was given to situation and drainage. The floor of the dwelling apartment was composed of a pavement of rough stones covered over with clay—and a cold damp floor it was. The cattle apartment had no pavement, so that the manure liquids and slop water percolated into the ground and at times found their way into neighbouring dwelling houses and even into the drinking wells. Many of the houses were built back-to-back and sometimes in rows three deep. Lighting was deficient and the windows, fixed either in walls or roof, were not made to open.

Some houses had round portholes in the roof at the top of the wall which might be opened or closed at pleasure; these served for lighting and ventilation at the byre end of the house, though occasionally they were present also at the living end. Draughts coming in through the roof and walls, and the blazing peat fire in the centre of the middle apartment, helped to keep the air in motion, but the smoke from the fire frequently filled the upper portions of the room and, there still being no chimney or other outlet as a rule, it pervaded the whole atmosphere of the house. From a sanitary point of view such houses had the gravest of defects: it amazed visiting doctors that infectious diseases were ever absent. Yet generally the inmates compared well in physique, general well-being and immunity from serious disease with those more favourably situated. Tuberculosis was the most prevalent enemy.

In 1879, improving leases were offered to those who were will-

(*above*) Sheep shearing: the first stage to Harris Tweed

(*below*) Natives of Shawbost, Lewis, engaged on wool dyeing, c 1910

DYEING WOOL - NATIVES OF SHAWBOST - ISLE OF LEWIS.

(*above*) Bales of imported Scottish wool on the quay at Stornoway for the Harris Tweed industry

(*below*) Dyeing wool in a Stornoway mill

ing to put their houses into better condition. The leases required, *inter alia*, that the thatch was not to be stripped off or removed for manurial purposes; that the byre was to be a separate building; and that the dung was to be removed regularly to a distant dung-heap. A Sanitary Inspector's Report for 1896 noted that the new houses being erected were following the old traditional patterns. And though the introduction of statutory requirements did bring real improvements, as late as 1902 it was reported: 'The insanitary houses and the impure water to which the people have long been accustomed, would lead an enquirer to expect a high death-rate. That is not so, however. The island is occasionally visited by epidemics of measles, or whooping-cough, like other parts of the country; and there are sometimes outbreaks of dung-fever—a preventable malady—but altogether the general health is good."

The Sanitary Inspector's Report for 1898 described certain water supplies in the island as 'little better than cesspools for surface soakings'. And five years earlier the water supply of Cromore was 'merely a few holes dug out amongst the arable land next to the houses; and polluted with the manure dissoved off their arable ground; and in some cases contaminated with liquid sewage percolating through the soil from their houses.' In 1893 an outbreak of typhoid fever in some townships in Uig was traced to the contaminated stream whose water was used as a drinking-water supply. Improvements in the water supplies were eventually put into effect, with a marked decrease in the ailments which the people had come to expect as normal to their way of life.

The rate of infant mortality was high. The weaklings died young. Only the strong survived to withstand the insanitary surroundings. A peculiar form of disease was associated with the island: it seized a child about the fifth night after its birth and was consequently called the 'fifth night's sickness'. According to medical opinion this was infant lockjaw *(tetanus neonatorum)*. The doctor of Lochs in 1892 reported that it was common among the infants of his parish, being 'most frequently met with in those dwelling houses where sanitation in its most rudimentary form is entirely ignored; where we have to walk to the fireplace in the centre of the mud floor through tons and tons of decomposing organic matter or manure.'

The island, for all its ills and chills, had a high birth-rate and a low death-rate. Martin Martin (1695) declared: 'It is a general observation of such as live on the sea coast that they are more prolific than any other people whatsoever.' In some areas of the island the birth-rate was as high as 35 per cent with a death-rate of about 12 per cent. The longevity of the islanders is well known, a fact confirmed by a glance any week at the Deaths columns of the *Stornoway Gazette*, regularly recording the decease of octogenarians, nonagenarians and some reaching their century.

In 1795 the island had only one surgeon. In Stornoway, 'Inoculation is performed here with success by the skill and attention of Mr Robert Millar, Surgeon.' Later, another doctor came to Stornoway, who attended to the sick in all parts of the island. By the turn of the century there were resident medical officers in each parish, with five doctors in practice in Stornoway.

Just after the turn of the century, there was a medical club in the north of Harris. This had been formed by the proprietor, Sir Samuel Scott, whose crofters were supposed to pay 5s per annum and cottars 2s 6d; this subscription covered dependents. In return, Scott guaranteed the salary of a medical officer, thus securing the services of a resident doctor in the district. But there was apparently considerable reluctance to call a doctor, whether the patient belonged to the club or not. The salary of the district Medical Officer of Health was £35 per annum, and from the North Harris Club he received some £200. Scott also provided him with a home. Dr Fletcher reported in 1906 that a complete change had taken place in the diet of the people within the memory of the older inhabitants, whose accounts of what they called new diseases and lowered virility he found very interesting. Good, plain wholesome diet 'has been replaced by cheap stuff, of questionable quality and purity. To this change there is another nondescript article which goes by the name of tea, in the use, or rather abuse, of which they are quite intemperate and from which they extract the last dregs by boiling. The result is disastrous to the strongest digestive system.'

In 1892 'a well-equipped medical and surgical hospital was

an urgent necessity for the island of Lewis', and a committee was appointed to collect funds, the subscription list being headed by Lady Matheson; for a period of three years donations flowed in from all parts of the world. The Lewis cottage hospital was opened on 1 February 1896, starting with only fifteen beds; the number was increased to twenty in 1915. An extension was opened in 1925, and the hospital was provided with a surgeon and an ambulance. Another extension in 1929 was the result of a gift of £3,000 from Mr John Bain, of Chicago, a Lewis son who was President of no less than fourteen banks in the Mid-West. The Lewis Sanatorium was started in 1926.

Tuberculosis was at one time in the island's history a disease that caused many deaths and much sorrow. About 1930 an Assistant Medical Officer of Health was appointed, Dr R. Stevenson Doig (who died in 1965), who spent his career-life in Lewis stamping out what was called in the island the 'white scourge'; he lived long enough to see the introduction of preventive medicine and the decline of the killing and crippling diseases he found on his first years in Lewis.

In dental health, progress has, as in so many areas, been reversed. At one time the island teeth were so well known for their strength and beauty that a film was made by the Army for showing to audiences considered in need of dental-health education. In 1966 the picture had changed: a survey revealed that 95 per cent of Lewis children were in need of dental treatment. The mainland addiction to sugary foods has spread.

As distinct from the island's general medical services, centred on Stornoway, the psychiatric services are based at Inverness. What was formerly the Inverness District Asylum, now called Craig Dunain Hospital, is the only mental hospital in the Highlands area, with a few long-term beds in the Institution at Lochmaddy; the general hospital at Stornoway conducts monthly outpatient clinics. Over the area served, the rate of admission to Craig Dunain Hospital is around 3·3 persons per 1,000 of population, compared with a figure of 4·68 for Scotland as a whole, 5·5 for Lewis and 2 for Harris.

The drink problem and Lewis's relatively high rate of admissions to mental hospital both stem from the background of the people; Lewis can be taken as representative of the Hebrides and the Highlands in general. The incidence of involutional melancholia, occurring mainly in middle life, is high and, to quote one expert, 'It would seem profitable to consider the states of fear and distress with which it has been associated.'

Those in Harris and Lewis aged fifty or over have their recollections charged with little else than disaster. Not only did the island lose an abnormally high percentage of its young men in

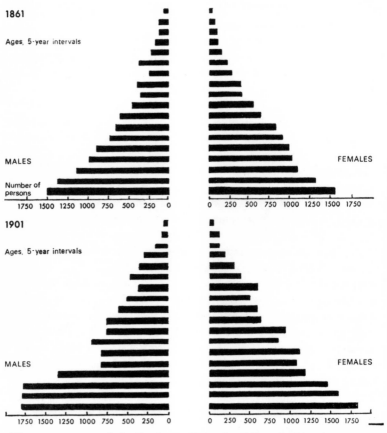

The age structure of the Lewis population in 1861 and 1901, showing the trend toward ageing as the younger elements emigrate (age scale 5-90 years reading from base)

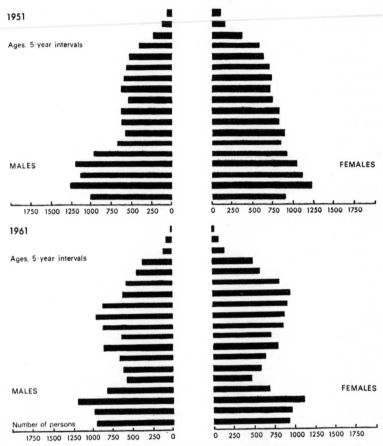

The age structure of the Lewis population in 1951 and 1961. The trend shown over the forty years 1861-1901 has strengthened and consolidated, so that the 1961 population is middle-aged

the 1914 war, but some 200 of those who survived the holocaust were lost in the wreck of the *Iolaire* on New Year's morning, 1919 —the first morning of the first new year of peace, literally within sight of home. Again, the effect of emigration was a loss, in many small communities, of a full generation. Where religion is strong and thrice-distilled, there tends also to prevail a state of mind which dwells on guilt and, where people are accustomed to ex-

149

press themselves in terms of religious values and ideas, the fear of having committed unforgivable sin. The normal adjustments, reflections and mental stocktaking of middle life are possibly more readily precipitated towards depression in an emotional people prone to serious thought. This brings of course a concomitant spectrum of problems in an area where in general a man is expected to take a dram and stand it; both nature and nurture are relevant factors. In the words of Cunningham Graham (1899), the medical adviser finds himself 'preaching teetotalism, that is for others, but himself taking his glass of whisky for the reasons which have been so cogently set forth by St Paul the Apostle to the Caledonians.' For those who comment in isolation on a community's indulgence in alcohol, one must quote a Gaelic proverb: *'Tha smuideag fhein an ceann gach foid'*—Every peatend has its own smoke.

From the earliest times the Western Isles have indeed been regarded as supporting a population with an uncanny predilection for spiritous liquors. To a certain extent the spirits were needed by ill-nourished crofters to keep out the damp and cold when on the moors or at sea; and people in a depressed economic or mental condition will anywhere seek refuge in alcohol or other available drugs—forgetting the old Gaelic proverb 'Better the little fire that will warm than the great fire that will burn.' The evil effects of drinking have certainly at times been serious: in 1869 Sir James Matheson addressed a circular letter of remonstrance to his tenants, indicating that those guilty of misconduct were liable to be deprived of their holdings. In 1920 a vote was taken in Stornoway under the Scottish Temperance Act, with the result that the town went 'dry'; three years later the poll was upheld. Then in 1926, with a majority of 84, Stornoway went 'wet' again.

But the 'drink question' has been given undue prominence and dragged out of its island context. For instance, Stornoway contains all but three of the licensed premises on the island (at Tarbert, Rodel and Carloway) and, as the chief centre for business and pleasure, must naturally attract anyone seeking refreshment.

CRIME

Serious crime is rare in the island, though it was not always so. Some light on the life lived in Lewis nearly two centuries ago is found in the old records of the Sheriff Court of Ross County. The first minute in the records concerns the appointment of George Munro, Writer in Dingwall, as the first Sheriff Substitute 'within the Island of Lewis'. The date is 1788. Munro's commission empowered him to sit 'in the town of Stornoway or anywhere else he may find most eligible at the time within the said Island of Lewis and hold Sheriff courts there, judge, decide and determine in all causes civil and criminal coming before him.' In those days a case might be raised in any of the county courts. In 1788, a regulation was made to save defenders from unnecessary trouble, hardship and expense in travelling to relatively distant courts where actions were raised against them; litigants had, before Munro's appointment, been faced with a long and hazardous journey to either Dingwall or Tain on the Scottish mainland.

The old Court Records date from 1788 and 1826 and record a number of interesting cases. Sheep-stealing was common, but other forms of theft less so; this is indicated by the fact that much of the Court Records are taken up with the minutiae of court appointments. In a case concerning wrecking, Lloyd's of London are mentioned as being represented in Stornoway as early as 1824 if not earlier. The defendants were fined £4 for destroying the mast of a ship found by them in Lemreway, in Lochs.

In a report dated 1902, a survey of crimes (offences against the person and offences against property) revealed that Lewis and Stornoway had good characters; considering the population number compared with the large influx of strangers to Stornoway during the fishing season, local people emerge as more law-abiding than the national average. Miscellaneous petty crimes were numerous enough, however: minor assaults, breaches of the peace and disorderly conduct, occurring mainly in Stornoway. Much of this 'crime' was traceable to drink. The island's first and only murder occurred a year or two ago.

THE PEOPLE

In common with other aspects of island life, the social side has undergone considerable change. The world has been brought nearer the crofter's home by radio, television and film screen, reducing the social need for meeting with neighbours and friends for the ceilidh. The ceilidh was once the principal means of recreation and instruction. There is no precise English equivalent for it, and it may be loosely described as an 'at home' to which all are welcome. It may be held in any house; in the past, the favourite resort was a home where the head (*fear an tigh*—man of the house) was an intelligent, communicative man; and if he had a number of eligible daughters so much the better. Ceilidhean were held after nightfall. Old tales were told, and songs sung, and public questions of the day were discussed. All women attending took with them an ample amount of work, sewing or knitting, to see them through the evening. Ceilidhean nowadays tend to be more organised, taking the form of popular 'concerts' which did not take root in the island until the turn of the century, though they were a common way of entertainment on the mainland at the time. Social life in the past was thus very intense, and was a natural evolution from the basic desire to forget the day's work and to have some pleasure of a kind.

The pattern of recreation facilities has since become fairly varied. Films came early to Lewis, or rather Stornoway; the first Picture House was located in Keith Street, and presented both films and stage turns. A new Playhouse was opened in 1934 with *The Good Companions* and *Falling for You*, starring Jack Hulbert and Cicely Courtnedge. Films in the rural districts were a rarity, however, until in 1946 the Highlands & Islands Film Guild came into existence to bring the magic of the screen to scattered communities. This body ran several mobile cinema outfits in the deep crofting areas, until the advent of television in the region killed it off in 1971. While it existed, however, the Guild provided an essential service to remote communities and brought not only the world to their doorstep but ensured that they felt part and parcel of a much larger scheme of things.

The first television service in Lewis began in 1959, 'piped' by an enterprising radio firm in Stornoway; its customers receive both BBC and Grampian Television programmes.

Some youth organisations are represented on the island. The first troop of Boy Scouts was connected with the Stornoway YMCA and was founded by forty boys in 1921. Founded (in 1912) on the island's close association with the sea was the Boys' Brigade (Naval), later to become the Stornoway Naval Corps and the Stornoway Boys' Naval Brigade. Its objects were to provide instruction in drilling, signalling, seamanship and first aid; and to foster a spirit of manliness and comradeship among its members. The founder was Canon H. Anderson Meaden, of the Episcopal Church in Stornoway (St Peter's). During the first war the boys acted as signallers at the Stornoway Battery.

But the provision of some organised recreational facilities for young people on the island has long been a thorny question. After the first world war, the Rector of the Nicolson Institute, Stornoway, proposed that village halls be built for village education and recreation. This scheme was never fully realised—except at Sandwick, just outside Stornoway—mainly because of the strength of puritanical opposition. This attitude has been breaking down, however, and it is now generally realised that the wealth of any community is based on its youth. Most of the efforts to set afoot activities for young people began after the second war; the work was hard and challenging with not a few failures on the way; perseverance has won to the extent that there is now a full-time youth leader. Most of the cultural and recreational activities are to be found in Stornoway, with a full range of interests. Evening non-vocational classes during the winter are also widely attended for a variety of subjects.

In 1965, an excellent Youth Hostel was established at Stockinish, Harris, with the help of the Inverness-shire Education Department. In its first season it recorded between 600 and 700 visitors (1,070 bed-nights). Also involved in the establishment of the hostel was the Harris Society of Social Service; practical help was given by the 2nd Stornoway Boy Scouts, who made a wall map, cleared up grounds and shifted furniture. A group of English enthusiasts have in previous years arranged a hotel at Rhenigidale, Harris (see Chapter 9), which provides for some fifty to eighty visitors each year, but there is nothing similar in Lewis. Hostellers who visit Stornoway can do little more than march through the town to the mail-boat, or else return to Harris by the next bus.

As might be expected, the reading tradition is strong, stemming from a natural desire to learn and from the fact that the ceilidh could only partly satisfy the need for mental stimulation, not to mention the need to alleviate loneliness. A century ago three books were to be found in many island homes: the family Bible, often a massive volume clad in hairy calfskin, *Turus a' Chriosdaidh (Pilgrim's Progress)* and *Gras am Pailteas* (Bunyan's *Grace Abounding*). As horizons became wider a public library was set up in Stornoway in 1907 (see Chapter 8); a library was in fact established there earlier, before 1897, but it was not a free one. In round figures, the 15,400 people of landward Lewis (Lewis excluding Stornoway) borrow some 70,000 books annually, though of course the actual readership figures are higher, books borrowed being passed round the family and exchanged with others until the 'mobile' calls again. The mobile library service was established by the Ross & Cromarty County Council in 1955 for rural villages in thirty-one school districts.

ISLAND EMIGRANTS

For all that the island is a tight-knit community, paradoxically it breeds many men and women whose destinies are not worked out within the confines of its own shores, but at the ends of far horizons. This is typical of most Highland areas: some who leave them make a mark on other societies often greatly exceeding the size of the community they left behind. Many 'great' people are also directly descended from a crofting ancestry; minds and spirits bred in the Highlands and Islands have potential for development not always apparent on native soil but sometimes fully realised in alien surroundings and conditions.

Harris and Lewis have contributed their share, and still do, to the general weal of skill, ability and intellect in all fields of human endeavour. For centuries, the export of brains was normal. Possibly the best known is Sir Alexander MacKenzie, who discovered the MacKenzie River; he was born in Stornoway in 1764, in what was known as Luskentyre House, at the corner of Kenneth Street and Francis, where Martin's Memorial Church now stands. Another MacKenzie, Lt-Col Colin MacKenzie, was born in Stornoway about 1754 and went to Madras in 1772 as a cadet in the Engineer Corps under the East India Company. In India, MacKenzie followed a career of high professional distinction,

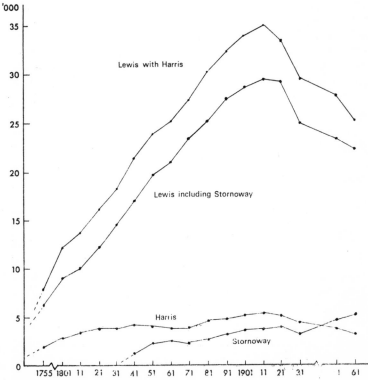

Population trends *c* 1755 to 1961 for the island as a whole; for Lewis, including Stornoway; for Harris; and for Stornoway. The population peak occurred in 1911. The dip in the Stornoway curve was due to the effects of emigration, as is the more pronounced dip in the island curve. Stornoway's curve in 1961 was on the upward trend, due to migration from the landward parts of the island into the town. Over the past 150 years, however, population mobility within the island has been virtually nil; movement has been emigration rather than migration

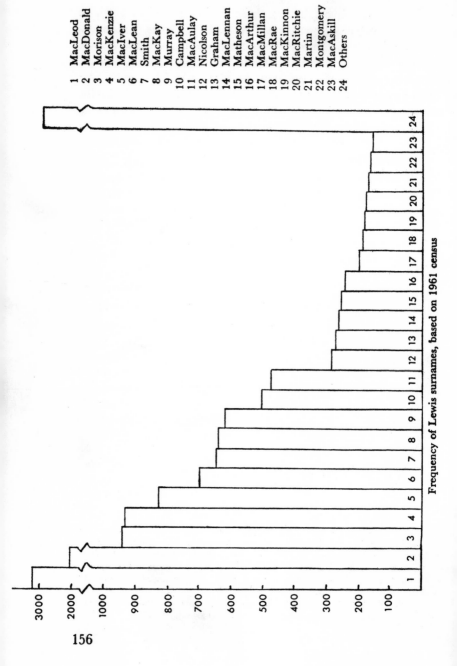

Frequency of Lewis surnames, based on 1961 census

1 MacLeod
2 MacDonald
3 Morison
4 MacKenzie
5 MacIver
6 MacLean
7 Smith
8 MacKay
9 Murray
10 Campbell
11 MacAulay
12 Nicolson
13 Graham
14 MacLennan
15 Matheson
16 MacArthur
17 MacMillan
18 MacRae
19 MacKinnon
20 MacRitchie
21 Martin
22 Montgomery
23 MacAskill
24 Others

surveying Mysore (40,000 square miles), a work of great difficulty, and ultimately becoming Surveyor-General of India. Though not island-born, Thomas Babington MacAulay, the first and only Baron MacAulay of Rothley, was an issue from the very heart of the Hebrides. He was only one generation removed from Gaelic-speaking ancestors. His grandfather was born in the Manse of Harris, and a great-grandfather in the far-off parish of Uig, in Lewis; a great-grandmother was born in the old Manse of Stornoway.

The MacIvers of Liverpool were a Lewis family who took a leading part in the development of regular steamship travel across the Atlantic and in the foundation of the Cunard Line. The brothers David and Charles MacIver first operated with passenger ships (the City of Glasgow Steam Packet Company, 1844) on the Clyde coast. Before that they ran a petty smack between Loch Roag and Campbeltown. Kenneth Morison, the founder of the Railway Clearing House, was born in Stornoway in 1805; in an unusual field there was Aeneas MacKenzie, who scripted many Hollywood films; W. E. Gladstone's mother was a native of Stornoway; and the last of the tea-clipper skippers was Captain Murdo Stewart MacDonald, who skippered the *Sir Launcelot*. Yet another local boy who made good is R. M. MacIver, who left Stornoway at the age of sixteen to make a journey, first to Edinburgh University and then on to Oxford, Canada and America. He has in his lifetime collected eight Honorary Degrees, became Lieber Professor of political philosophy at Columbia University, and President, and then Chancellor, of the New School for Social Research.

S TORNOWAY is the only real town in the Hebrides. Some even say that it is the only real town in the world, as its basic living patterns are those of the countryside from which it sprang. It has always been held in high regard by the islanders. In the past it was regarded as one of the most important places in the civilised world: a saying attributed to a primitive native has passed into a proverb: *'steornabhagh mhor a' chaisteal —baile 's modha 'th'air an t-saoghal gu leir ach Bail'-ath-Cliath an Eirinn—'s iongantach nach eil an Righ fhein a' tighinn a comhnuigh ann!'* ('Stornoway the great, with its Castle, the largest town in the wide world, except Dublin in Ireland; surprising it is that the King himself does not reside therein!') The affectionate name for the town is 'Portrona', Port of Seals, which it is. A son of Stornoway once said, 'The founder of Portrona must have been some sea rover with a good eye for a refuge from the storm and the peril of his calling. No matter what winds rage outside, within the bay the mariner may drop his anchor, furl his sails, and take his ease.'

When the Vikings first came to the western isles of what was later in history to become Scotland, they found a sandy spit of land on which they could beach their longships in a sheltered bay. It was, however, more than a haven; it was a place in which to settle down and rear the first of many generations. Later the Norse-derived MacLeods took advantage of an outcrop of rock beside the beach to build a fortress. Later again a greenheart pier, and later still a concrete wharf, have given the town the outward symbols of economic and social significance.

Stornoway owes its origin to the Stornoway Beds, a sedimentary formation much younger than the Lewisian gneiss. These Beds have had two effects. First, their existence and formation allowed a deep indentation, giving a good harbour with a protecting isthmus not far way. The harbour itself is due to the erosion of these rocks about intrusions or dykes of more resistant crinanite. Second, the better nature of the soil derived from the weatherings of the sandstones and conglomerates has aided reclamation and cultivation.

In the long years of its existence the town has been a focal point of island history, fanning out to many corners of the world, where it has been merged with the wider history of Britain, the Commonwealth and elsewhere. Detached as it was from the rest of Scotland by the Minch, Lewis often went its own way. In the reign of Queen Elizabeth, when England and Sweden plotted against the Scottish crown, the emissaries of these countries met in Stornoway. Later, in April 1719, a council of war was held in a room in Stornoway to plan the overthrow of the Hanoverian dynasty of Britain; included in the assembly were the Earl of Seaforth, the Marquis of Tulibardine, George Keith, the hereditary Earl Marshal of Scotland, and his younger brother James, who was to become the famous Marshal Keith. Prince Charles Edward, though not setting foot in the town, looked at its twinkling lights from across the Bay, at Arnish, while his pilot tried to obtain a boat to take the royal fugitive to France.

The harbour has seen many kinds of ships on its waters. In the twenties, the *Metagama*, the *Marloch*, and the *Canada* came to take away almost a generation of young Lewis folk to the new lands across the seas, because their own island could not support them. The *Iolaire* sank within sight and sound of the harbour mouth and dragged about 200 Lewismen with her into an island memory. The *Cervona*, of Dundee, dropped her anchor just by Arnish lighthouse in July 1904, carrying survivors from the emigrant ship *Norge*, sunk at Rockall with appalling loss of life. The *Victoria and Albert* visited Stornoway in September 1902, the first visit to the town by a reigning monarch. That was a great day, the result of a letter from Provost Anderson of Stornoway in which he pointed out to His Majesty, King Edward, that with less than 30,000 inhabitants Lewis had 2,300 men in the Royal Naval Reserve, trained at the local Battery, the largest in Britain. There were also 1,100 men in the Seaforth & Cameron Militia, all of whom volunteered for foreign service in 1899, and 900 of whom did garrison duty in Egypt. Between 300 and 400 Lewismen served in the various regiments at the front in South Africa, and over 300 in the Royal Navy.

In 1796 there were sixty-seven slated inhabited houses in the burgh, twenty-six of which had been built since 1784. Before this date most of the houses followed the constructional pattern of those found in rural Lewis. In 1838,

> Stornoway was, within the last twenty years, only a small fishing village, but from the spirited and patriotic exertions of Lord Seaforth, the proprietor, and the grant of irredeemable feus for building, it has become a place of considerable importance as a fishing station. It has a post office; and a packet sails regularly once a week with mail and passengers. No place in the North of Scotland, and in an insulated situation also, has made more rapid strides at improvement, both in a domestic and commercial point of view, than Stornoway.

COMMUNICATIONS

Mention of the sailing packet indicates the tedious manner in which mails came to the town for subsequent distribution in the island. Letters went by mailcoach north to Dingwall, thence by mail-gig west to Achnasheen. Because there was no road from Achnasheen to Poolewe, about thirty miles away, they had to be carried on horseback. The weekly sailing packet then picked up the bags, for which cargo the owners were paid £150 per annum. A letter from London to Stornoway cost 1s 5½d; the smallest enclosure made it double that amount. The mail-packet was often held up by bad weather. It was a wind-blown sailing ship that brought Stornoway the result of the Battle of Trafalgar and the death of Nelson, an event in which a number of Lewismen also took part and died; in St Columba's churchyard at Eye there can still be seen a Trafalgar officer's gravestone. A fortnight after this news arrived, the packet from Poolewe brought its stale message.

In 1844 seventy boats, ranging from 15 to 150 tons, were working out from Stornoway. The *Gazetteer* for Scotland for that year says, 'The grand trade of the place consists in the exchange of the produce of the fisheries and the kelp shores, for British manufactured goods and foreign produce. There is a Branch office of the National Bank of Scotland, two friendly societies, four inns, and so many as about a score of dram shops.' The annual burgh revenue was £17 3s and the expenditure £15 17s 6d. The town boasted ten streets, a saw mill, a mill for carding wool, a corn mill, a very large malt barn and mill, and an extensive distillery. These buildings were constructed 'in a style not much inferior to the best buildings of their class in Scotland . . . A stranger on arriving at it by any route, or from any quarter, is surprised to see so large and flourishing a place in so remote and uninviting a corner. Its broad field of houses, its capacious bay, and spacious piers, its occasional crowd of shipping, and stir of trade and gaiety, and the vicinity to it of the aristocratic mansion of Seaforth-lodge, render it a striking and very welcome relief to the prevailing dreariness, sterility and inertion of the rude country in which it is nestled.'

In 1901, when the West Highland line was opened, the return fare from Mallaig to Stornoway by MacBrayne's steamers was 14s 6d. One could go from Glasgow to Stornoway by steamer for 31s 6d return. A *Guide* for that year indicated that Stornoway had three hotels, six churches and a Court House, singled out for specific mention for some reason. A Ross-shire *Directory* of 1914 describes the Nicholson Institute as one of the four Junior Student Centres in the county. Its Leaving Certificate results were the best in the north of Scotland, with a total of 95 higher and 234 lower passes, and no less than 20 passes in Higher Science.

Stornoway is a Burgh of Barony, dating from 18 October 1607. It had, of course, been a town of sorts long before the Charter was granted by James VI; the Charter was executed under the Great Seal conveying equal shares to three of the leaders of the Fife Adventurers. Under the Police Act of 1862 Stornoway became a Police Burgh. A bank agent in the town was appointed first Chief Magistrate on 31 December 1863. Under the 1892 Act, the designation 'Town Council' superseded that of 'Burgh Commission' and the Chief Magistrate assumed the title of Provost, the senior and junior magistrates becoming known as senior and junior bailies. The present Municipal Buildings were opened in 1929. The previous building was only an idea in 1897; it took

161

shape when Dr Andrew Carnegie offered to contribute £1,000 towards the construction of a library, provided the town adopted the Public Libraries Act. This was done, and the Council decided to incorporate the library into a larger structure, erected at a cost of £11,000 and opened in September 1905 by Lord Roseberry. Carnegie increased his contribution to £3,500, with other large donations from public-spirited industrialists of the time (eg Coats of Paisley, who also financed school libraries in the island).

Being a seaport, the sea has been basic to the town's livelihood. In the eighteenth century trade flourished between Stornoway and the Baltic, Scandinavia, Holland, France and the north of Ireland; and in the first half of the nineteenth century, fish was exported as far away as ports on the Mediterranean. The advent of steam killed the Stornoway sailing craft. At one time in its history, the shipyard (at Matheson's Patent Slip, now the site of the textile mill) turned out many fine vessels. The scent of tar and pitch, the crunch of a busy grindstone, the shaping of a ship's timbers, the steaming of her planks, the driving of pins and bolts, the music of mallet and caulking-iron, the buzz from the saw-pits and the riggers aloft, all gave the town a sense of at-one-ness with the waters in the bay. Then there were the schooners, brigs and barques of foreigners who put in for repairs or for merchandise. It was a time of glory that has now gone as surely as the sail has disappeared from the high seas. Ship-masters, ship-owners and sailors all added colour and variety in the streets as they mingled with the local population—which numbered 1,000 in 1801. Stornoway captains were world-known for their skippering : Mac-Leods, MacIvers, MacKenzies, Ryries, MacLeans, Morisons, Allans. These were the names that were once reeled off to be paired with the famous ships of the day : *Sir Launcelot, D. L. MacKenzie*, and *Assaye*.

While large numbers of its sons were sailing the high seas, many in ships of Stornoway origin, the town began to take on the first look of a port, with piers. On 9 August 1864, Sir James Matheson subscribed the instrument which took the Stornoway Harbour Commission into being. The following year, on 29 June 1865, the Commission was incorporated by Act of Parliament. Matheson had shown a great interest in the development of the existing harbour facilities. But his efforts to promote the town as an industrial centre were opposed, a dispute arising between him and parties who claimed interest in the quays which already existed; his action to set up the Harbour Commission and to acquire the Crown's interest in the shores of Stornoway Bay *ex adverso* found local opposition. He succeeded in quelling the doubts and the resulting counter-actions, however, and then, with the decks cleared, the Commission lost no time in getting developments under weigh. Authorisation to borrow up to £10,000 was obtained and work put in hand on building a timber wharf, 150 ft long, filling in certain areas for fish-curing and other purposes, and constructing sheds, works buildings and warehouses. By 1881 this work had been completed and, with the expansion of the herring industry, the Commission sought to increase its borrowing by £20,000; in 1892, further powers for borrowing the sum of £55,000 were sought and obtained. By the turn of the century all the works authorised by the 1892 Order were completed : they met the berthing needs of the fishing industry and also the reclaimed areas on South Beach, North Beach and the Cromwell Street quays were used continuously during the season as fish-curing stations, proving essential factors in the development of that industry.

Before the 1914-18 war ended, Lord Leverhulme had become proprietor of the island and, as such, a member of the Harbour Commission. He proposed further development of the existing facilities, to line up with his scheme for establishing Stornoway as a centre for industrial activity based on fishing. Plans were prepared, and a permanent way for a railway (linking the canning factory at Inaclete with the harbour) was formed. But the scheme did not materialise before he abandoned Lewis for Harris. Before he left, however, he conveyed free to the Harbour Commission considerable property round the inner shores of Stornoway Bay. At this stage the Commission promoted a New Harbour Order, passed by Parliament as the Stornoway Harbour Confirmation Act, 1926, in which provision was made for the increase of the Commission's borrowing powers (up to £70,000) and the setting up of a contingency fund of £10,000. Further improvements were put in hand. Another Order (1947) was obtained and the present harbour facilities are the result of this, with a causeway to Goat Island—a small snippet of land off the Newton shore—the King Edward Wharf extension to give a depth of 24 ft at low water, and the construction on Goat Island of a slipway and slipway jetty.

The present facilities are valued at several million pounds; they evoke, however, a blank stare of disbelief. Much of the industry for which the quays were first envisaged has now gone. The days of 300-400 fishing boats and the landing of several thousands of crans each week, with the attendant bustle and activity, belong to the past. The harbour remains reasonably active, with a considerable extent and variety of shipping: general traffic due to the Harris Tweed industry has continued to increase in recent years. The introduction of the ferry service direct from Skye to Tarbert, Harris, has however had perceptible effects.

When Leverhulme parted company with the people of Lewis, his gesture of farewell offered the island to its people. This brought into being an agency for the people of Stornoway and its rural areas, so that they were in effect in control of their own future to a degree unique in Britain. The Stornoway Trust was formed in 1924. Besides property in the burgh and its suburbs, including the Castle and its park or policies, the Trust owns virtually the whole of the landward area of the parish, from Arnish Moor northwards to the township of Tolsta. Freshwater fishings are in its hands, as are the resources of the sea and inshore fishings on the shorelands. During its first five years the Trust was faced with a growing deficit, though this was redressed partly through agricultural derating and partly through the registration of the Trust as a charity, thus exempting it from income-tax demands.

The Town Council, the Harbour Commission, and the Trust have overlapping representation, for harmonious work on behalf of the community. Indeed, by the conditions of the Deed of Trust drawn up by Leverhulme (in 1923-4), the Stornoway Trust must include the Provost of the burgh as its chairman, together with magistrates and councillors. Throughout the years of its existence, the Trust has sought to increase its usefulness, but at the beginning decisions were often taken piecemeal. Portions of the property were sold, one such causing legal history. The chief garage proprietor in the town applied to use for his business a site he had purchased at a road junction near the western end of the town, close to the principal new housing schemes and opposite the main gate leading into the Castle grounds. It was a mistake in planning, and public disapproval began to make itself felt. The Trust, in an effort to redress the situation, sought to distrain the garage proprietor from extended use of the area. The parties went to law, and the case was fought through the courts until, in the House of Lords, the Trust finally lost and had to pay a bill of some £4,000, equivalent to a fine of £4 to £5 from every family in the burgh. The Trust drew its lesson, and since has formulated a more alert and constructive policy.

The town is well served by its shopping centre, with multiple stores jostling for custom with smaller private business concerns. Prosperity for all, however, depends on the well-being of the Harris Tweed industry. If there are recessions, as there have been in the past, the tills rattle spasmodically. Also standing to suffer are others such as the bus companies (who provide the efficient town services and link up Stornoway with the rural areas), the builders and the haulage contractors. In the ever-present climate of unemployment it is the policy of the mills to employ male labour, despite the fact that women would be cheaper. The mills, run by natives or by Lewis-born incomers of the second and third generation, realise a social obligation in recognising that in Lewis the strong tradition is that the man should be the head of the family in every sense. The mills also carry a proportion of surplus labour to offset the unpredictability of those workers who, with crofts to look after, occasionally have to take a day off 'at the peats' or some such activity. This is another of the island's distinctive traditions.

On Cromwell Street is the shop of James MacKenzie & Sons Limited, dealing in hardware, furniture and china. Nothing unusual in that, at first sight: yet it is another unique aspect of life in Lewis, being conducted as a charity for the benefit of, among others, the aged and infirm persons of Stornoway. The business was established in 1830, on its present site. In 1964, the then principal shareholder presented the building and the business as a going concern to a trust which was set up to receive the gift and whose first object is to assist aged and infirm residents in the burgh. In effect, all profits earned by the shop are passed to the trust for distribution to those in need.

Almost half the houses in Stornoway were built by the local authority. The Town Council has never been afraid of rooting out unfit houses. By 1937, under the 1930 Slum Clearance Act, one person in four in the town lived in a council house. The housing schemes, though large, have still that element of community with personality, something often lacking in newly developed areas of other towns and cities. The Council also supports private housing by taking up sites, clearing and servicing them and then feuing them to private owners. The rents policy is to have no housing deficit beyond the statutory rate contribution (which works out at between £6,000 and £7,000 per annum). The Council's tenants co-operate with rent collection to a unique degree : collection figures are something like 99 per cent and on occasion 100 per cent. A vigorous housing policy is important to the town, as its population is now over 5,300 and still growing, mainly at the expense of the rural areas. Development plans at present envisage a 1981 population of about 9,100 persons within the parish boundary and including the burgh.

Stornoway is an island town and is an island's town : its rhythms of life are those of the island, regular and timed by nature, but with an added syncopation—the result of an urban outlook. In this context, Gaelic is the language, though English is the lingua franca. Deeper still in the methods used for communication is a kind of patois based on Gaelicised English, Anglicised Gaelic, with some other words that defy investigation into their origin. Many words find their natural forebears in Scots, American and the maritime tongues of Europe, which might be expected in view of Stornoway's importance as a sea-port of significance a century or two ago. The Stornoway language, as spoken by true-born natives, recognisable anywhere by another native, reflects the life of the cosmopolitan, sea-faring people.

Apart from its industrial opportunities, Stornoway has many of the more sophisticated urban facilities that people everywhere seem to crave, particularly with regard to education. The senior secondary school, the 'Nicolson', has had since its inception a formidable academic record. Back in 1907 work from the school was included in the educational section of an International Exhibition held in Christchurch, New Zealand : this was appropriate because emigrants from the west Highlands, notably from Harris and Lewis, were among the pioneers of New Zealand education a century ago. In 1957 new extensions were opened, costing about £300,000 and making the school the largest of its kind in the Highlands area. It is co-educational, its primary and junior secondary departments taking only Stornoway children and its senior secondary department catering for those from both Stornoway and rural Lewis. Many board out in the town during the week, returning home at weekends.

In providing social facilities, the town has placed itself in the position of an agent for those things deemed necessary for life, and is a middle-ground between the rural repression of the Free Church and the city abandon of the mainland, with resulting dilemma. The public houses, the cinema, youth clubs, dances and juke boxes are all in direct opposition to the preaching of the Free Church. The result is tension between the town's desire to act as a host for tourists and its wish to fulfil its duty on a religious plane; to instance this, the Stornoway Sabbath is less strict than the Lewis Sabbath. In keeping with the rest of Lewis, social standards are extremely high. Home is the centre of life, as it always was; the sense of community and communal responsibility is there. Divorce is practically unheard of, and the incidence of crime, as such, is extremely low.

9   *A HARRIS VIGNETTE*

L IKE a Siamese twin, Harris is joined to Lewis in eternal geographical union. The junction is at the body, however; the head of each island part has always been clear to develop its own characteristic. Thus, Harris has a quite separate personality which has risen above the common factors it has with Lewis. Both have the same historical origin : the Clan Leoid. This clan comprised two leading tribes, the Siol Torquil (Mac-Leods of Lewis) and the Siol Tormod (MacLeods of Harris). Tradition has accorded to them a common progenitor, Leod; though by the time history in the Western Isles was old enough for the recorder's pen the two tribes, or families, were distinct and independent of each other. Malcolm, son of Tormod MacLeod, head of Siol Tormod, had a charter from David II for the lands of Glenelg, on the Scottish mainland, which he and his successors held from the Crown. Also included in his possessions were Skye and Harris, which came to his family after the forfeiture of the Lords of the Isles in 1493. The MacLeods of Harris have, rather strangely, their clan seat at Dunvegan on Skye, and are more commonly known as the MacLeods of Dunvegan or Skye, though 'of Harris' is their correct title.

The MacLeods were, by and large, good proprietors. They held much fertile land and the clan was reasonably wealthy. Tenants' rents were paid mostly in Scots money and, to a lesser extent, in such farm produce as oats, barley, cheese, butter, wedders and marts, and in labour services. When times were hard for the tenants their rents were often 'eased' by the chief in the hope that subsequent years might prove more fruitful and that the eased rents would be paid in time. In 1705, a bad year, MacLeod actually cancelled 'eases' owing by the Harris tenants, as a gesture to them. In 1712, when some disaster had visited the St Kildans (the islands belonged to MacLeod), their chief provided them with a new boat and the islanders were allowed a two-year delay in payment of their rents to help the recovery of the community.

Lands were not allowed to become waste; in 1710, a Roderick Campbell in North Uist was paid to come north and settle in the island of Ensay, Sound of Harris.

It is significant that much of MacLeod's rents was paid in money rather than produce, for it emphasises the great value of the cattle trade in the Highlands, in which Harris played a not insignificant part—that is, compared with neighbouring Lewis. It was sound economy for the Highlands, and far in advance of the theories of the so-called 'improvers' of a later age. The rents of the MacLeod estates were collected by chamberlains, and part of the work of Malcolm Campbell, the chamberlain for Harris at the beginning of the eighteenth century, was the ferrying of Harris cattle to Skye. In Rodel, MacLeod had a 'keeping house', which probably consisted of rooms for the chief while in Harris; there was also a brew-house.

To introduce more efficient communications and to interconnect all the small Hebridean islands of the estate, a boat was purchased for a Lauchlan MacLean in 1705; he was empowered to maintain a regular ferry between Harris and Skye. This also operated between the mainland of Harris and the populated islands in the Sound, such as Berneray, Ensay, Killegray and Pabbay. In religion the estate was Presbyterian, and MacLeod had the burden of providing both suitable residences for the ministers and the communion elements. As mentioned earlier, the Rev Aulay MacAulay, the great-grandfather of Lord MacAulay, the English writer, was once minister in Harris.

The first half of the nineteenth century saw great changes in the ownership of the various islands comprising the Outer Hebrides. MacLeod of Harris retained Harris until the end of the eighteenth century, when it was purchased by a cadet of the family, a son of Sir Norman MacLeod of Berneray, for £15,000. This son, Captain MacLeod, who had made a fortune in the Far East and ploughed some of it back into his native soil, was the man who introduced fishing as an industry to the Harris people. In 1834 the Harris estate passed to the Earl of Dunmore for £60,000. Dunmore sold north Harris to Sir Edward Scott in 1868 for £155,000. In 1919, Lord Leverhulme bought south Harris and St Kilda for £36,000.

A HARRIS VIGNETTE

Linking the present day firmly with an ancient past is the probably fourteenth-century church of St Clement's, at Rodel. It is an outstanding building, and the only considerable architectural monument in the Western Isles. Built of rubble, dressed with schist, and freestone which must have been imported for the purpose, it is cruciform, with nave, choir and two transeptal aisles, the fabric being covered with carvings and sculptured panels. The first mention of the building is made by Dean Monro, in his account of his tour of the Western Isles, *c* 1549. In the first half

St Clement's Church, at Rodel, Harris

of the sixteenth century it was extensively repaired by Alexander MacLeod of Harris, who died in 1547 and whose remarkable tomb it houses. He prepared it nineteen years before he died; reckoned to be among the finest in Scotland, elaborately wrought, and with Latin inscription, nine sculptured panels cover the rear wall of the alcove, with the recumbent effigy of an armoured warrior with ornamented bascinet and camail lying below. Round-toed sabbatons cover the warrior's feet, which rest on a lizard-like beast, a lion standing guard at head and feet.

Other tombs inside the church include that of Mary MacLeod, a bardess of the seventeenth century who was also governess to the young MacLeods at Dunvegan. She was probably the first to compose what may be called the 'court' song, in simple words and in the 'strophic' verse-form of rhythm and assonance enjoyed by all Gaels since her time. Her last elegy was composed to Sir Norman MacLeod of Berneray in 1705.

So far as personal characteristics are concerned, there is a marked difference between the Herrach (Harrisman) and the Leodhasach (Lewisman). Their Gaelic dialects are different, the Harris pronunciation being much softer, with an attractive singing lilt. And Harris Gaelic has fewer words of Norse origin. The main reason for this difference has been a topographical one: before a road was cut, the mountain barrier of north Harris divided the inhabitants of the two parts of the same island, who developed in their own distinctive ways.

The character of the land of Harris has also had much to do with the difference. Harris for the most part is infertile, with great expanses of rock outcrops. The east side of the island is torn in shreds by fiord-like sea-mouths; the west coast is slow-moving, with large expanses of sand and machar-land which look out over the Atlantic breakers rolling in from a sea that is oceanic in appearance and in fact. From early times the Harris folk have had to work hard to scarify their snippets of land to make it fertile. Regular increases in population forced them to cultivate land extending up to 500 feet above sea level in some places, in the form of hard-won lazy-beds. After the clearances early last century, when the more fertile lands on the west coast were taken over for the formation of sheep farms, the people concentrated on the eastern side of the island, and on some of the higher ground in the west.

On Lord Leverhulme's death in 1925 the ownership of large tracts of Harris passed to absentee landlords. After this, some of the lands which had been cleared a century earlier were purchased by the Government and broken up into crofts again, enabling some of the indigenous population to come back to make use of the more fertile lands of the west. There are some 550 crofts in Harris, with 29 regulated common grazings; the total

171

acreage of regulated common grazings amounts to 65,000 acres. The working units (as distinct from crofts) in Harris are classified according to the arable acreage; the majority have up to 10 acres arable land. Less than 250 acres of land have been improved.

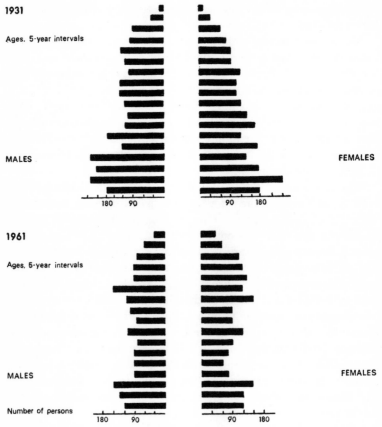

The age stucture of the Harris population in 1931 and 1961, showing the decline in numbers and rise in age

There are four districts in Harris: North Harris, with its islands; the Bays of Harris on the east coast; the Leverburgh area, with the islands of the Sound of Harris; and the west coast. North Harris is mountainous country, dominated by the Clisham

(2,620 ft); grouped around this are the lesser peaks staring stark and treeless to the skies. At the feet of these hills are the small villages straggled along the shores of West Loch Tarbert. Much of this area is owned by the proprietors of Amhuinnsuidh Castle, a magnificent structure built by the Earl of Dunmore in the last century; the hills lying north of it are rich in red deer. The road past the castle trundles on until it peters out at the far-east village of Hushinish, beside a glorious scimitar-like curve of silver sand. Beyond Hushinish is the Island of Scarp.

The road along the shores of East Loch Tarbert ends at the village of Kyles Scalpay which overlooks Scalpay island. The Bays of Harris hold in their crevices the scattered groups of houses here and there, where an inlet of the rocky coast affords some anchorage and where a patch of ground is suitable for cultivation. Tortuous, winding footpaths have been gradually replaced by narrow roads connecting the townships. Lack of sufficient remunerative employment has led to considerable depopulation. Fifty years ago the population of the area was just over 5,400; it is now about 2,900.

The south of Harris is better known for its association with Lord Leverhulme. Obbe, later Leverburgh, became the centre of his schemes. He built a large pier, huge kippering sheds, houses for the workers, roads and lighthouses, and blasted away underwater rocks which hindered free navigation. The bulk of this work was complete in 1924, but when he died (in 1925) his successors, in the cold light of economics, decided to close down the embryo industry and realise its assets. The harbour works had cost £250,000; they were sold for £5,000 to a demolition company. Leverhulme's memorials are still to be seen. The west coast of Harris is now becoming known for the long stretches of shell sand and the green machar-land beside it, a true delight for the tourist seeking isolation.

Tarbert is the central village in Harris, with a population of about 400. It is a thriving community, nestling at the foot of Beinn an Teanga and at the head of the sheltered anchorage of East Loch Tarbert—sheltered from the prevailing south-westerly winds and from the Atlantic storms. The car ferries give direct contact with the Scottish mainland, via Skye, and Tarbert also has direct or indirect communication with Glasgow, Stornoway and North Uist. In summer a thrice-daily bus runs to Stornoway, and once a day a bus makes the round trip of East and West Harris. The township, linear in pattern, east to west, includes six-teen shops which cater for most of the needs of the population within reasonable travelling distance; it also has two cafés, a post office, a licensed hotel, a hall for social functions, a masonic hall and two churches. The Sir E. Scott School here is the only secondary school in Harris with an academic stream. Most of the working population is employed in the service in-dustries, the professions and the tweed industry. Tarbert was a fishing port of some significance in the past, and is now a re-fuelling point for ships.

The absence of organised industry on a large scale, such as Lewis has, is a factor which tends to bring nearer to reality any desire on the part of Harris natives to leave their native soil. There are small pockets of industry, but these are only dabs of easing ointment on the excessive unemployment sore of 27 per cent. The main occupation is of course crofting, the income from it being augmented from a variety of sources. Some crofters concentrate on the production of Harris Tweed, perhaps using the wool from their own sheep; the natural dyes from the lichens which grow on the rocks and from other plants are still used occasionally. Others specialise in knitwear. Recently shell-craft and wood-turn-ing have been added to the traditional crafts, with a view to the tourist market. Fishing, of course, plays a part in the economy in some communities. The interest of such organisations as the Scot-tish Country Industries Development Trust has been concen-trated on the potential in shell-fish processing, and the production of knitwear on a larger scale than exists at present. Road-work gives employment to about thirty men, but is of course seasonal.

An apparently bright light on the employment horizon showed itself in 1965, with the opening of a quarry at Lingerbay. The mineral quarried was anorthosite, a white granite used as an abrasive in cleaning products. A 99-year lease was taken out by a subsidiary company of William Robertson (Shipowners) Limited, Glasgow. But the quarry was closed in 1967 due to lack of orders.

Fourteen employees were directly concerned, with another six in the services sector.

The potential of the tourist industry is only beginning to be tapped. MacBrayne's drive-on drive-off car ferry, with a capacity of 50 cars and 600 passengers, makes two or three trips a day between Uig in Skye and Tarbert, the journey taking less than two hours. The mainstays of tourist accommodation in Harris are the Tarbert and Rodel Hotels, both well appointed and owning fishing rights for salmon and trout. Sea fishing is another tourist attraction. Crofters participate in the holiday trade by offering full board or bed and breakfast, caravans, caravan sites or vacant lets.

An interesting tourist venture has been started at Rhenigidale. A rough, stony track, one of the most tortuous and exciting in Britain, takes its leave from the main road over a ridge. It twists and turns in and out of gullies, over cliffsides and across the steep heather-clad slopes of the Toddum, a dramatic little hill of 1,730 ft which protects Rhenigidale village from the Atlantic gales. The seven-mile track is the only marked route, though crofters take a shorter way to the north over pathless bogs; the local postman makes a round of about 60 foot miles in the week, walking this track and on to Tarbert three times in all weathers. The village relies on its sheltered harbour with a good natural rock pier : most communication is by water, all food and fuel coming that way. In past times every household owned a boat for lobster and shell fishing to supplement both diet and finances. Today the interest in fishing has declined, as has the population. But in 1946 Mr Herbert Gatliff paid his first visit to Harris, discovered what the island had to offer, and started a campaign to convince hostelling interests of the need to make some investment in the Western Isles. A croft house in Rhenigidale was in 1961 equipped as a hostel, and under what is now the Gatliff Trust it is maintained for hardy trekkers, the Scottish Youth Hostels Association making a grant for running costs. Many visitors have found that the place offers a degree of happiness corresponding with its remoteness from civilisation.

A HARRIS VIGNETTE

Scarp

Until 1972 Scarp was the most westerly inhabited island in Scotland, separated from the Harris mainland by a strait which is about half a mile across at its narrowest, coursed by strong tidal currents. The island is about three miles in diameter, rugged, especially in the north and west, with cliffs on all sides; the maximum altitude is nearly 1,000 ft. On the east side lies a tiny marginal belt of good land, machar and soil; on this green shelf, about one-third of a mile long, were all the crofts of the Scarp settlement. Many stand deserted, and abandoned lazy-beds in sites beyond the present settlement indicate a denser population at one time. The island's population-carrying capacity was severely limited by the minute amount of land available for tillage: of a total of about seven square miles only half a square mile can be used. Climatic conditions and soil type also restrict the range and quality of crops grown.

Scarp was originally settled about 1810 and was occupied by eight farming families who were reasonably comfortable. Not only did they have the island to themselves, but they had access to good pasturage on the Harris mainland opposite. About 1823 thirteen small townships between the head of Loch Resort, Harris, and Bunabhainneader were cleared, some of the displaced families coming to Scarp. Some emigration back to Harris took place in the 1840s, but when about 1868 the proprietor divided Scarp into sixteen crofts instead of the previous eight holdings, these were further divided by the people themselves, trying to accommodate their families and friends from elsewhere. In 1861 the population was 151; the peak was reached in 1881 with 213 persons. In 1951 it was 74. Communication with the Harris mainland is by boat, plying between two stone-built jetties.

The local economy was essentially a subsistence one, with self-sufficiency in such products as potatoes, turnips, cabbages, oats, milk and fish. After a break of some years lobster-fishing has recently been reinstated as an occupation. Oil lamps are the only lighting, though a few houses have piped water. The small shop stocks essential household items, and extensive use is made of mail-order. A few years ago a telephone to the mainland was supplied, much valued in emergencies.

Scarp in fact has a small place of its own in the history of communications: on 28 July 1934 one of three British rocket-mail experiments (for which special stamps were printed) was held there. The inventor of the rocket, Herr Zucker, was later to become prominent in V-rocket work during the second German war. Herr Zucker personally conducted the firings. His rocket, a large cylinder with pointed nose, something like a heavy shell, was 3 ft long and weighed 30 lb, with capacity for several thousand letters. The motive force was ordinary high explosive contained in a large cartridge about 18 in long; the device was designed to burn with a series of rapid explosions and produce a flight speed of 1,000 mph. The firing apparatus was a flimsy wooden structure providing a runway rising at an angle from the ground, an elastic sling giving the rocket an initial impulse. The first rocket was fired on Scarp, to the mainland: it exploded prematurely and most of the mail was damaged. The postmaster applied to the backs of the damaged covers a three-line cachet in violet: 'Damaged by first explosion at Scarp—Harris.' In order that this mail should be actually flown, it was re-transmitted by the second firing made in the opposite direction, Harris—Scarp. The whole experiment was deemed a failure, however. The route taken by the mail addressed to Kirkwall was unique; rocket, ferryboat, motorcar, mail steamer, railway train, and finally by Highland Airways to Kirkwall.

Depopulation in Scarp was encouraged by the lack of employment prospects, and centralised education, of the type which has already played havoc with remote rural communities elsewhere, is felt to be a black cloud darkening the future. Much the same problem faces Scalpay Island, mentioned later. Children are removed from their home environments for higher secondary education at a central school: for Harris children this is at Portree, Skye. Many islanders argue that the scheme tends to destroy the family unit, urbanising the children so that they become unsuited to, and with no inclination for, rural life. Some sympathy must be felt for the education authorities, of course, as the provision of adequate educational facilities in remote spots becomes increasingly difficult.

In its time Scarp has contributed more per head of population to the professions than has any other community of similar size. The last of the native Scarp population left the island in November 1971 : two families totalling seven people. The island has now attracted the attentions of a hippie community.

Scalpay

Scalpay Island, on the east side of Harris, was formerly occupied by two or three tacksmen in succession before being 'crofted out'. About 1843 the Harris factor settled twenty crofting families who managed to make a fair living there, but five years later another twenty families were added; some had been evicted from the island of Pabbay in the Sound of Harris. This led to some subdivision of the available land. The 1861 population was 388, but the figure rose to a peak of 624 in 1921; in 1951 it had declined to 541. It is now in the region of 450.

Island Scalpay is in fact one of the few places in the Highlands and Islands area in which the normal trends associated with remote regions are operating in reverse. The island despite its smallness—it is a mere 3 miles long and $1\frac{1}{2}$ miles across—supports a thriving and dynamic community and is the envy of its neighbours. Scalpay is retaining its young folk; and it boasts some of the finest homes in the Hebrides. From the agricultural point of view it is not greatly different from other islands in the Hebrides. Its forty crofts produce a good crop of oats; but less than 20 acres of the land are re-seeded.

The land being as poor as it is, the men of Scalpay have turned their faces to the sea—for a living, not for emigration. Scalpay has the largest number of full-time fishermen and a total of thirty-three boats, twelve of which are ringnetters of over 40 ft. Native enterprise is also shown in the ship-owning firm whose vessels carry freight and passengers to many parts of Scotland and on occasion to the Continent. A Harbour Association was formed on the island in 1966 to work for local amenities for fishermen and the community generally—in particular for a landing stage in the North Harbour. The lighthouse at Eilean Glas, Scalpay, was in fact erected as long ago as 1788; for a long time it was the only lighthouse in the Western Isles. In 1792 it was described as 'one of great utility to the numerous shipping that frequent this channel [between Skye and the Long Island] on their voyages to and from the Baltic'.

The independence of the islanders again appears in their attitude to the education facilities provided for their children. In 1949 Scalpay parents staged a school strike in protest against the delay in the construction of a road to the school. At present the island has a junior secondary school but in 1966 the Inverness-shire County Council Education Committee proposed the transfer of the island pupils to the school at Tarbert; this would mean each child rising early in the morning to face a trip across Scalpay Sound and then a road journey to Tarbert. The inevitable protests against this proposal were rooted in its deeper implications. The school roll on Scalpay (70 pupils) has maintained a remarkable level of continuity over the years, reflecting the general prosperity of the island. Forced attendance at a central educational facility, the islanders maintain, will introduce an unsettling urban element into their children's adult views.

The smaller islands

To the west of Scalpay, in East Loch Tarbert, is the one-square-mile island of Scotosay. Its population was 14 in 1861, none in 1881, 18 in 1891, 15 in 1901, and 20 in 1911. In 1921 7 males and 12 females lived there, but none permanently since.

On the west of the Harris mainland is a high rocky island, four miles by one, called Taransay. In 1549 Dean Monro described it as being 'well inhabit and manurit', a place where people delved with spades, and with good barley and corn, and fishing. There are two old chapels and a burying ground on the island. The population of Taransay has declined to a handful through the years; its peak was 76 in 1911.

The Sound of Harris is 'a chaos of rocks and islands', so numerous that they cannot easily be counted. Some are mere pinpoints of rock; others once supported small populations. Nearest to the

179

southern shore of Harris is the verdant arable island of Ensay, two miles in circumference. The peak population was 15 in 1861, but in 1951 and 1961 there were two men (seasonal shepherds). Just south of Ensay is Killegray, two miles long. The south end was uncultivated, though a good source of peat; five people lived on Killegray in 1861, 3 in 1911 and 1921, 5 in 1931 and none in 1951. An 1865 report mentions that there was only one house on the island, so the population must have been one family only.

Four to five miles west of Killegray is a low-lying, fertile island of about four miles by $1\frac{1}{2}$. This is Bernera Harris which, though lying nearer to North Uist, is included in the civil parish of Harris. It still carries a fairly large population. Until the early eighteenth century it was occupied by a tacksman at one end and a community of crofters at the other. Later there was an influx of people evicted from Pabbay and the mainland of Harris. Some clearing of families from Bernera itself took place. In 1861 the population of Bernera was 315; it rose to 524 in 1901. Three schools were open on the island in 1865 : an SSPCK school, a Gaelic School Society school, and a 'female industrial school' supported by the SSPCK and 'taught by a venerable Highland lady in receipt of a salary of £8 per annum'. The school was housed in, to quote an 1865 report, 'the oldest dwelling in the Long Island, and was at one time inhabited by persons of distinction. In the outer wall is a marble slab bearing this inscription : "Hic Natus est/Illustris Ille/ Normannus MacLeod/De Bernera/Eques Auratus." (Here was born that famous man, Norman MacLeod of Berneray, a distinguished knight.) This illustrious personage and his brother, Sir Roderick of Talisker, were both knighted by Charles II for distinguished services . . . A grandson of Sir Norman became known in the annals of the Bench as Lord Bannatyne.'

Three miles north-west of Bernera is Pabbay, also in the parish of Harris. At one time Pabbay was a rich green island, the 'granary of Harris', and supported a considerable population. Early last century it was inhabited by 26 families (about 100 people), who lived in comparative comfort, and by 1841 the population was 338. But Pabbay was cleared of its people. Some emigrated to Australia, some went to other places nearby, such as Scalpay, Bernera and the Bays area of Harris. In 1858 only a shepherd's family was left. Pabbay is conical in shape, and about 2½ miles in diameter. In recent times drift and sea spray have damaged its fertility.

Just north of Pabbay is Shillay, one mile in circumference, where Martin Martin (1695) says he found sheep with the biggest horns he had ever seen. Whether Shillay was ever inhabited is not known.

10 THE OTHER ISLANDS

T HE continued evacuation of islands is a problem peculiar
to Scotland. In the eighteenth century some 8 per cent of
Scots lived on islands; today the figure is less than 2 per
cent. Island populations today account for about 30 per cent of
the total Highland (crofting counties) population. The difficulty
for most islands is the relationship between population density
and potential for economic development.

As though reflecting the relationship of man to man on Lewis-
with-Harris—keeping together in community for survival—the
other islands round the larger island mass have played some role
at one time or another in recorded history. Most of the socially-
significant islands of Harris have been described in Chapter 9.
Lewis has very few, and these are mostly far-flung oceanic outliers.

North Rona

To begin at the northern point of the Lewis parish, about 45
miles NNE of the Butt of Lewis is North Rona, a block of horneblende schist with pegmatite intrusions. Though the island has
never figured in any Census reports, since the Census began, it has
been inhabited from time to time. Of about 300 acres in extent,
it is cliff-bound and reaches 355 ft at its highest point. It lies in a
part of the Atlantic where a deep swell seems perpetual, and landings can be difficult.

Dean Monro comments: 'Towards the north northeist from
Lewis, three score myles of sea, lyes and little ile callit Roney,
laiche maine land, inhabit and manurit be simple people, scant of
ony religione.' The Dean's 'simple people' were no recent settlers.
They were in fact the continuation of a community which had
inhabited North Rona for at least 700 years previously. Tradition has it that the first inhabitant was St Ronan, who built a
small monastic cell or hermitage there some time during the
eighth century, but there may have been earlier inhabitants.

Though the island is but a great lump of rock, Dean Monro says that in his time an abundance of corn was grown, by delving only, and an abundance of clover-grass for sheep. The island also produced a fine bere-meal which the islanders stuffed into the skins of sheep and sent, as their rent or tribute, to MacLeod of Lewis, along with mutton and fowls.

Of St Ronan's Chapel, still to be seen and reckoned the oldest Christian building in Britain remaining in its original state, Monro says: 'As the ancients of the country allege, they leave a spade and a shuil [shovel] when any man dies, and upon the morrow find the place of the grave marked with a spade, as they allege.' In 1695 Martin wrote of Rona in 1680:

> The people repeat the Lord's Prayer, Creed, and the Ten Commandments in the Chapel every Sunday morning. They have cows, sheep, barley, oats, and live a harmless life, being perfectly ignorant of most of those vices that abound in the world. They know nothing of money or gold, having no occasion for either; they neither sell nor buy, but only barter for such little things as they want; they covet no wealth, being fully content and satisfied with food and raiment; though at the same time they are very precise in the matter of property among themselves; for none of them will by any means allow his neighbour to fish within his property . . . They concern not themselves about the rest of mankind except the inhabitants in the north part of Lewis. They take their surname from the colour of the sky, rainbow, and clouds. There are only five families in this small island, and every tenant has his dwelling-house, a barn, a house where their best effects are preserved, a house for their cattle, and a porch on each side to keep off the rain or snow. Their houses are built with stone and thatched with straw . . . When any one of them comes to Lewis, which is seldom, they are astonished to see so many people.

Then came tragedy. Somehow, probably off a wreck, a swarm of rats landed on the island and consumed virtually all the food. A few months later, some seamen landed and robbed the islanders of their only bull. 'These misfortunes and the want of supply from Lewis for the space of a year occasioned the death of all that ancient race of people.' Some years afterwards a new colony was sent to the island. In 1796, at the time of the *Old Statistical*

183

Account, there was one family there, that of the person employed by the owner to look after the livestock. The owner was a Ness tacksman who paid £4 sterling rent per annum. The island produce was corn, butter, cheese, a few sheep and sometimes a cow, and some wild fowl and feathers.

In 1844 Rona was evacuated, its last inhabitant being, in the seventh year of Queen Victoria's reign, the 'King of Rona', Donald MacLeod, who lived in almost prehistoric conditions. Rona was without inhabitants until 1884, when a last attempt at resettlement was made by two men from Ness. This was a self-imposed exile, after a difference of opinion with the minister of their parish; in penance, they hied themselves off to Rona. In 1885 a relief boat called and found both men dead, one from natural causes, the other from starvation and exhaustion after nursing his friend. By the fireside of their hut was a pot ready for the preparation of a meal they never ate.

Today, man's connection with the island is maintained by the small party of Lewis shepherds who each year make the journey to shear the sheep which still graze on the green slopes around the now-ruined village. Otherwise, only the occasional traveller now lands there. In June 1956, North Rona with its associated rock, Sulasgeir, was declared a National Nature Reserve on account of its importance as a breeding ground for colonies of oceanic birds—guillemots, puffins, kittiwakes, and fulmars—and for its seal colony.

Sulasgeir

Sulasgeir is twelve miles west of North Rona, a lonely rock in the Atlantic, bleak and grassless, and tunnelled by caves and gullies. The only life it has ever supported is seabirds—officially. Yet one of the old buildings is said to be a chapel and is called 'Tigh Beannaicht' (House of Blessing). According to Ness tradition, Sulasgeir was once used as a prison for sheep-stealers, and it is also said that Brenhilda, sister to St Ronan, was left on the island to perish. Yet another tradition claims that it was at this rock that Prince Charles Edward made his first contact with his Scots clansmen, when the ship that carried him to Scotland was spoken to by a Ness boat making for North Rona.

Dean Monro, in his 1549 account, refers to the vast numbers of wild fowl and mentions that the men of Ness sail there and stay for seven or eight days and bring back a boat full of dried wild fowl and feathers. The *Old Statistical Account* (1796) says: 'There is in Ness a most adventurous set of people who, for a few years back, at the hazard of their lives, went there in an open six-oared boat without even the aid of a compass.' The boat, says the *Account*, could not be pulled up out of the sea, and therefore, while some of the men worked on the birds, the others had to stay in the boat on the most sheltered side of the sheer-cliffed island. This custom of hunting young gannets (or 'guga') on Sulasgeir still continues. Under the Protection of Wild Birds Act, 1954, the gannet is protected by law, but so that the Ness men could continue their old custom, a Statutory Order was passed making a special exemption (from 31 August each year at the end of the close season) of the gannets on Sulasgeir. With North Rona, Sulasgeir is one of the great breeding grounds for British oceanic seabirds.

The Loch Roag islands

The one large inhabited island off the Lewis coast is Great Bernera, though technically it is not now an island, having been connected to the mainland of Lewis in 1953 by a bridge. It is part of the parish of Uig, as are the other islands in Loch Roag. Its population reached a peak of 730 in 1911, but has now fallen to about half that figure. Off the west of Great Bernera is Little Bernera, which in Dean Monro's time was 'inhabit and manurit', but which has had no population recorded since the 1861 Census. Monro describes it as full of rough little craigs, but with fertile earth between.

Also in Loch Roag are three islands which, now deserted, once supported families: Pabbay had 17 people in 1861, 9 in 1881, and none since; Vacsay had nine men in 1861, and none since; Orasay in 1891 had one man and one woman, but none since.

The Flannans

Belonging again to the parish of Uig is the group of islands known as the Flannans, or Seven Hunters, some twenty miles north-west of Gallan Head. There are seven main islands, all small, high and cliffbound, and a number of rock stacks and islets. All are uninhabited. Eilean Mhor, the largest, of 39 acres, has an automatic light. Dean Monro's description of the islands as 'nouder manurit, nor inhabit, but full of grein high hills and scheipe' still holds, for sheep are taken annually from Lewis to the grazing on the Flannans. Their name is said to be derived from the ninth-century St Flann, whose saintly influence was recognised during the centuries when men from Lewis visited the islands for their harvest of wool, wild fowl and feathers.

The Flannans were the scene of a great sea-mystery : the complete and utter disappearance of three men from the lighthouse at the turn of this century. In December 1900, the lighthouse, with its 140,000-candlepower beam 283 ft above sea level, was a year old. It had taken four years to build instead of the estimated two. All the materials had to be swung up piecemeal from the boats and hauled up the almost sheer 70 ft cliffs to the top. That month a passing ship, the *Archer*, noticed that the Flannans light was out; a message was sent to the Flannans shore station at Breasclete, Lewis, and the *Hesperus*, preparing to pay a Christmas visit to the lighthouse, got under weigh.

Its crew landed and searched the island, but found no trace of the missing keepers. In the lighthouse was an uncanny silence. The fire was dead. The clock had stopped ticking. The beds had been made up in the clean, clinical way of all sailors. And in the galley, the pots, pans and dishes sparkled their welcome to the searchers. In the lamp-room the lamp was cold. The wicks had been trimmed and the lenses polished. The logbook showed a last entry on 0900 hours, Saturday 15 December. In the subsequent investigation some theories were offered in explanation of the disappearance, but none quite fitted. The mystery remains, a haunting, unexorcised cloud hovering over the island.

The Shiant Isles

Turning to the east coast of Lewis, in the parish of Lochs are the Shiant Isles, about 4 miles off-shore, across the Sound of Shiant (Gaelic : charmed, enchanted). There are three islands in the group : Eilean an Tigh (House Island), Garbh Eilean (Rough

Island) and Eilean Mhuire (Mary's Island). The Shiants are the eroded relic of the same age of volcanic activity that formed the strange-looking columns of Staffa and of the Giant's Causeway in Antrim. The mass of cooling molten rock slowly crystallised and changed in composition : the early-formed crystals sank to the bottom, the later ones being found nearer the top. In 1845 one family lived on Garbh Eilean, the largest, which is joined to Eilean an Tigh by a low storm beach; but the family was lost, falling over one of the great precipices which are a feature of the group. In 1821, 2 males and 4 females lived there; in 1891, 3 males and 5 females; and in 1901, 4 males and 4 females. But in this year the last family upped and went to Tarbert, Harris; for one of its members, a girl of 21, it was the first visit to the outside world. Since then there has been no permanent population. Back between 1811 and 1821 a visitor to the Shiants had some hard things to say about the filth and darkness of the shepherd's dwelling in contrast with the 'loveliness of nature, the bright sand, the fair rock, the enamelled green turf, and the sweetness of the summer breeze'.

Records show that at one time in the islands' history some sixteen people lived there, working small crofts. The ruins of their chapel can still be seen. The author Sir Compton MacKenzie had the house on Eilean an Tigh renovated for a stay there, and later the islands were bought by Nigel Nicholson, author and publisher. Today they are used for grazing sheep.

St Kilda

The St Kilda group of islands, some 45 miles off the west coast of Lewis, belong to the parish of Harris. These islands have an extensive literature and can only be touched on here. When the population was evacuated from St Kilda in 1930, the move broke for all time almost 2,000 years of continuous island living; they were taken off at their own request, after much careful and serious deliberation by the St Kilda 'parliament'. Life in Hirta, the only island in the group with a permanent human settlement, depended on the seabirds that breed in their tens of thousands on the cliffs of Hirta and Boreray, and the great stacks of Stac an Armin and Stac Lee. The flesh of puffins, gannets and fulmars was the staple diet of the St Kildans; the oil and feathers were the vital exports that paid the island rent to MacLeod of Harris, the owner of the group. These exports also helped to pay for the purchase of such foodstuffs as salt, sugar and tea, and other items which the island could not itself supply. The St Kildans owned some hundreds of sheep, the wool being spun and woven into tweed, and a few cattle were also kept. But the seabirds were the foundation of the island economy.

The factor which led ultimately to the desertion of the island group was isolation. The community there was throughout its history undoubtedly the most isolated in the British Isles, though until the present century this mattered little to the St Kildans. All that was deemed necessary for the continuation of the community was that, once a year, MacLeod of Harris should send his factor over from Skye to collect the island goods that were to be sold, and to bring with him those provisions which would see them through another twelvemonth. However, as the demand for the island's products declined, communications became more important: to support the family a man had to leave to find work on the Scottish mainland. Large-scale emigration began in 1852 when thirty-six islanders (with State aid) left for Australia. Island life was punctuated by loss of life; boating disasters and cliff-falls in particular deprived the community of the vital male elements needed for survival. Tetanus infantus, known on St Kilda as the 'eight-days' sickness', strangled two of every three babies born; this disease ravaged the island for almost a century and again struck harder at the male sex. About 1810 the population was about 200, a definite overcrowding. By 1861 it had fallen to 78; in 1911 it was 80, and in 1921, 73. A decade later it was nil.

Isolation tended to make the St Kildans a human menagerie. With the improvement in boat services, St Kilda became a 'must' on tourist itineraries. The tourist trade took on an economic importance for the population after July 1877, when the *Dunera Castle* steamed north and west for a voyage to the 'romantic Western Isles and lone St Kilda'. The steamers continued to call throughout the three summer months annually for sixty years, their passengers eager to buy souvenirs: tweed, quern stones, spinning wheels, stuffed birds and eggs; indeed, anything to remind them, and to show their friends at home, that they had braved the hazardous Atlantic seas to visit St Kilda on the very edge of the world. The tourists were charitable, but this brought a psychological evil in its wake. In 1886, Robert Connel wrote: 'One cannot be long on the island without discovering the great moral injury that tourists and sentimentalists and yachtsmen, with pocketsful of money, are working upon a kindly and simple people.' It was estimated that the islanders collectively derived a profit of 5s from each of the 200 or more tourists who arrived during the short summer.

The new influx of cash into a community which required money as an exchange commodity because the original native produce was becoming less saleable, hastened the decline of effort to be self-supporting. The numbers of seabirds slaughtered steadily fell; paraffin oil replaced the traditional bird oil in St Kildan lamps. The need for daily work, to toil in fellowship with others, was dissipated; the islanders could purchase most of the food they required, provided communications with the mainland were maintained. The population was in any case dwindling, as St Kildans became more aware of 'the other life' available on the mainland of Britain.

Finally, on a misty summer's day in August 1930, at a cost to the nation of little under £1,000, St Kilda was left to the care and keeping of the changeless Atlantic. It is now preserved by the National Trust for Scotland as a crumbling monument to a small human tragedy of a kind that has been repeated, and will be repeated, in other small communities who cannot argue out the case for their survival in terms of economic viability. The island is now occupied by military personnel in connection with the Hebridean rocket range on South Uist.

St Kildans were described by Dean Monro, in 1549, as 'simple, poor folk, scarece learned in any religion'. In 1698, Martin Martin published *A Late Voyage to St Kilda*. He went there in the company of a minister who had been summoned to the island to denounce a certain false prophet who had risen among the 180 inhabitants (pretending he was an emissary of St John the Baptist). Martin found, as did later visitors, that the island economy and the quality of its life were closely dependent upon its birds, even to the extent that the St Kildans used their observations of the flights of birds both as compass and as omen for good or evil. Martin speaks of the islands with amusement and admiration. He indicates that the community was backward in some ways : they were illiterate, and wondered naïvely at the newcomers and their manners. 'The inhabitants of St Kilda are much happier than the generality of mankind, as being the almost only people in the world who feel the sweetness of true liberty.'

In May 1877, when the local tourist trade had hardly started, HMS *Flirt* sailed from Greenock with food to relieve hardship among the St Kildans, and an officer of the Highland & Island Agricultural Society on board reported that 'Tobacco was what they invariably asked for'. The ordinary diet of the island consisted of, for breakfast, porridge and milk; for dinner, potatoes and the flesh of fulmar, or mutton and, occasionally, fish; for supper, porridge when meal was plentiful. Seabirds' eggs, from March onwards, also formed a staple food. Tea was taken once or twice a week and the islanders were reported to be 'rather fond of it'. There were eighteen inhabited houses, sixteen of which had zinc roofs, two being thatched huts. The sixteen new cottages had been erected about 1863, 'and are certainly much superior to the inhabitations of the same class of tenants anywhere in the Western Isles'. All were well furnished, peat was used for fuel and there were two watches and one clock on the island. There were some seventy-five islanders; most of the men were old, and only two of them were unmarried, with twelve spinsters still to choose from. All read the Gaelic Bible. The men were mostly tailors, shoemakers and weavers; every house had a loom. They made all their own clothing, the men also making the women's dresses, and a good deal of blanketing and tweed cloth was made and sold. Nearly every house had a spinning wheel and a large pot in which the yarn was dyed. The women were expert knitters. Each croft and house was rented at £2 annually, sheep being charged for at the rate of 9d per head; these charges were usually paid in kind.

Feathers of the sea fowl formed the principal export of the island. The factor paid 6s per stone of 24 lb for black feathers; and 5s per stone for grey. For these he received, in Edinburgh or

Glasgow, between 7s and 10s per stone. For tweed made on the island, 27d to 30d was received per yard; for blanketing, 28d. Cloth was measured by the 'big yard', which was 49 inches. The factor bought cheese at 78d per stone of 24 lb. The prices paid by the islanders for commodities imported included 25s per boll for meal and oats; 3s per cwt for salt; 7d for coarse sugar; 5s per lb of tea; whisky cost 4s per bottle; and tobacco was 5s per lb. Leather for soling boots cost 24d per lb; for uppers 27d. Bonnets for the men were 4s each; cravats, 3s. Physically, the islanders were in good condition at the time of the *Flirt's* visit, with an average height of 5 ft 6 in, though they showed a tendency to flabbiness. The prevalent illness was rheumatism, with dyspepsia running a close second.

11   ISLAND LIFE

AS one might expect with an island that is not obviously sur-
rounded with water, life in Harris and Lewis is lived out
by an amalgam of communities somewhat similar to those
found in very large cities, with defineable districts and recognisable boundaries. The island is too large for any physical feature
to demonstrate that it is unconnected with a larger land mass.
One looks to the horizon, down the coasts, at the satellite islands,
and concludes that if indeed it is an island, the separate elements
which combine to make an islander must be found elsewhere
than in the landscape. And so they are : in the people, their way
of living, their economic problems, their attitudes, and their own
consciousness of the fact that distance over the hills and the moors
to the sea is significant, in that one eventually comes to the end
of a road or track; or that a river or stream runs itself out for
ever into the sea. Harris and Lewis is the biggest of all the 'small'
islands off the shores of Britain, and has been fortunate in its
size : large enough to support a significant number of people who,
despite emigration, have managed to maintain their numbers
reasonably well and who are now making efforts to reduce emigration and its effects on the island communities to a bearable level.

Because it is an island, however, external influences are felt
like cold winter winds. The 1966 seamen's strike was an example;
Government intervention was needed to supply essential goods.
After the strike many questions were asked. All had their roots
in the island's dependence on the outside for not a few of the
necessities which could be produced on Harris and Lewis itself,
with either its own resources or the resourcefulness of the island
folk. To be short of fish, for instance—and this occurred—while
the seas around the island were teeming, was unhappy history
repeating itself, a harking back to former times when starvation
levels could have been avoided by looking around for the means
to harvest the crop lying around. The strike also threw into relief
the question of the viability of crofting as a full-time occupation.

192

Research into markets and more co-operative effort, into better use of the land with less dependence on subsidies and grants, is scheduled for the Western Isles Crofters' Union.

Fishing as an industry, though now receiving the necessary shot in the arm by the establishment of the nucleus of a local fishing fleet, is still bothered with the perennial problem of poaching. The Minch remains one of the great fishing areas of Britain, but, it is argued, its fertility is forever being depleted by fishing inside the three-mile limit. This limit was originally chosen because it was the effective range of a cannon ball about two centuries ago. Fish, however, when they choose their spawning grounds are uninfluenced by the range of eighteenth-century artillery, paying far more attention to the nature of the sea-bed, which varies as much inshore as it does offshore.

POLITICAL ORGANISATION

In 1918, the Outer Hebrides became a separate Parliamentary constituency known as the Western Isles, a recognition of their geographical position in relation to the many other islands off the west coast of Scotland. Before this constituency came into being, Lewis formed part of the County of Ross & Cromarty for Parliamentary purposes, while Harris and its own islands of Scarp, Taransay, Scalpay and the isles in the Sound of Harris were included in Inverness-shire.

For the purposes of local administration, however, Lewis still forms part of Ross-shire (part of Ross & Cromarty), with its centre at Dingwall, the Ross & Cromarty county town; while Harris, North Uist, South Uist, Benbecula and the Barra Isles belong to Inverness-shire, and are administered from far-away Inverness. The Lewis association with Ross-shire is a historical one. When the boundaries of the Earldom of Ross were changed in 1661, Lewis went with Ross as part of the possessions of the Lords of the Isles. The present districts recognised for administrative purposes do not in fact greatly differ from the divisions, or parishes, set up after the creation of the Bishopric of Ross in the twelfth century, the Lewis parishes being Stornoway, Barvas, Uig and Lochs. The County Council attends to finances, education, roads, public health and general administration, and has offices in Stornoway. Stornoway itself is largely looked after by a Town Council which deals with the property of the burgh, makes and administers byelaws and imposes burgh rates. The police are under County administration, each burgh paying an annual contribution for their services; the law is administered by a sheriff-principal and two sheriff-substitutes, one of whom holds court in Stornoway. Each parish has a local committee of management.

The political history of the Western Isles, and no less Harris and Lewis, reflects the agrarian troubles. Before 1917, when Lewis was a Parliamentary part of Ross & Cromarty, and Harris part of Inverness, the electorate was both Liberal and Radical; traditionally there has been a significant anti-Tory vote. In 1917, the Boundary Commission for Scotland set up the Parliamentary County of Inverness and Ross & Cromarty, with three divisions: Inverness, Ross & Cromarty and the Western Isles. In 1918 the Western Isles voted for the first time as a Parliamentary constituency of its own, and showed a predominant Liberal sympathy; the returned candidate was also standing for the reform of the Land Law.

In the General Election of 1923 a Liberal candidate was again returned, with a repeat performance in 1929. In the latter election however, the Socialist came in second place. In the crisis or scare election of 1931, the Labour Party did not contest the seat, which was won by a Liberal-National candidate opposed by a full-blooded Conservative. In 1935 the Labour candidate, a native of Lewis, was returned with a 1,345 majority. This Member retained his seat through all subsequent elections losing it only in 1970 to a member of the Scottish National Party, who became a lone Home Ruler in the House. Labour, Conservative and Scottish National parties are represented in the constituency, with a small Liberal showing. The revision of local authorities has given virtual autonomy to the Western Isles.

PUBLIC SERVICES

The lack of adequate social and public services has been cited by some authorities as a factor encouraging people to leave the island; but islands in isolation must carry a population of suitable numbers and age structure before they can support even a minimum of amenities. In the Western Isles, Stornoway used to be the only community to have a semblance of the services taken for granted in similar towns on the British mainland. The elements of commerce, industry, education and religion were established there initially, to spread with characteristic slowness first to the immediately accessible areas and then to remoter regions. Though many parts of the island are now at least within practicable travelling distance of the social and public services expected in urban communities, some townships have yet to see one or another of them within their own boundaries.

The Stornoway Gas Light Company was formed in 1840 by Sir James Matheson, with a capital of £350. The plant consisted of one horizontal retort which produced about 1,000,000 cu ft of gas annually. The old buildings still stand, and the plant now has three vertical retorts with an annual production of just over 40,000,000 cu ft. Rural areas use Calor gas, introduced to the island in 1935.

The public electricity supply has of course made the greatest impact on the island as a whole. Electricity was known in the island long before the public supply arrived, generated privately by individuals, hotel concerns or public authorities. One of the first plants of significance was installed in the second municipal building in Stornoway (the first, built in 1905, was destroyed by fire in 1918), and was driven by a gas engine. In 1919 Lord Leverhulme installed an electricity plant in Lews Castle, which also had a private intercommunication system. While this work was being done Leverhulme proposed to give electric lighting to the town. Other buildings with their own plant included the hospitals and the mills, which were turning to electric motors for driving their line shafting, the power take-off for spinning and carding machinery.

In 1929 an electricity supply company, with a capital of £12,000 was proposed, the Stornoway Electric Supply Company being registered in 1932. Its financial fortunes were chequered, though revenue was rising slightly by the time the second world war began. In 1948, on nationalisation of electricity supplies, the company gave way to the North of Scotland Hydro-Electric Board. In that year there were 1,063 consumers, all within the Stornoway burgh boundaries. With its social remit, the board started on bringing power to rural areas, even where uneconomic. Lighting in the crofting townships was mostly by oil lamps, mainly the hot-mantle type (the 'Tilley'), but by 1960 the number of electricity consumers had reached 8,124, and the present number is about 96 per cent of the potential. Harris received its supply in 1954. The generating station is at Stornoway and employs diesel-engined units as prime movers, with an annual output of some 22,000,000 units. In August 1960 the Gisla scheme came into operation, the island's first hydro-electric plant; designed to produce some 2,000,000 units annually, it harnesses the waters of the Gisla River, which flows out of Loch Grunnabhat in the parish of Uig, Lewis. The station has a capacity of 540 kW. The other hydro-electric scheme is at Loch Chliostair in North Harris, planned to produce about 2,400,000 units annually.

The provision of water and drainage is still on the drawing boards for a number of crofting townships, though work is progressing for others. The Uig water scheme has cost some £100,000, a relatively large sum for a small population and amplified by similar work for drainage schemes. This scale of public expenditure must continue if people are to stay in their native villages and not migrate to Stornoway or leave the island altogether. Stornoway's new water scheme has cost something in the region of £160,000, but is vital if the town hopes to attract industry. The original burgh water supply was started in 1846 by Sir James Matheson and a few businessmen. The capital of the Stornoway Water Company was only £800, but it gave the town a gravity-feed supply from the nearby Loch Aridh na Lic long before many larger places on the mainland had considered such projects. Heavy floodstorms destroyed the old dam in 1933, and a new waterworks at Loch Mor a Starr was opened in 1937. As Stornoway extended the old loch had outlived its usefulness; for many years there had been difficulty in getting water to the higher parts of the town, particularly during the heavy fishing seasons when the fishermen drew off large quantities.

As in other Highland areas, some of the island's problems have become so deeply entrenched as to be intractable. They have been the *raison d'être* of so many commissions and committees of inquiry that their existence is now almost forgotten by the islander —if indeed he ever understood their nature. Some results have been seen, such as the Crofters Act of 1886 which gave Highland crofters security of tenure, perhaps the most valuable measure of the last century or two. But somehow all things have not progressed so well since that date; at any rate not so fast that crofting, for instance, is now seen to be an economic form of land use of benefit to both local community and nation at large. Many problems have been virtually ignored by successive central Governments; at least, remoteness seems to qualify a topic for the office 'pending' tray. It has yet to be fully realised that the island, with other Highland communities, is part and parcel of the area generally administered from London and Edinburgh, and merits as much attention to its welfare as other European governments, such as Norway, give to their remote mainland and island communities.

As usual, charity and self-help begin at home, and one of the most dramatic changes in island life has been the result of the agricultural revolution of recent years which is changing once-brown moors to lush green pastures: reclamation by re-seeding. This revolution is still going on. Lewis crofters in particular are showing the way, with other Highland crofting areas following suit. The change in the Lewis scene is being emphasised by the planting of shelter-belts of hardy trees and the first of the new plantations of timber-producing trees. These show the promise of the future: a lively future for a lively community. The fishing industry also has a future, brighter on the horizon than it has been for many a poor year. The Harris Tweed industry, the staple employment-source in Lewis, is maintaining its ability to retain the interest of the market. And tourism, once a perfunctory and casual affair, promises to emerge as a useful sector in the economy. There are, in addition, many small pockets of native initiative and enterprise which, given sufficient encouragement

197

and practical support, could win through to make marks on the island scene.

A significant event occurred in 1964: the establishment of the Highlands & Islands Development Board. This was Britain's first regional development authority run by members who are either full- or part-time. The Board is grant-aided and has two broad functions: to improve the social and economic condition of the Highland people and assist in making the region more significant in a national context. The Board's attention in the Western Isles has been concentrated in the expansion of the fishing industry and the development of tourism. In both these fields there has been a considerable success: upwards of 100,000 visitors per annum visit the islands; and a fleet of over thirty boats, equipped with the latest gear, operate out of Stornoway.

Also in 1964 was produced the Development Plan for the County of Ross & Cromarty. So far as Lewis was concerned, the Plan was based on an average decrease in population of some 1,500 persons for every year in the future of the island. This, if carried to its logical conclusion, will see complete desertion in fifteen years or so! However, even if nothing further is done to halt emigration, particularly in the landward areas of the island, the population will remain around a stable 15,000. The County Development Plan contains much food for thought, but as with most county plans, does not indicate actual development projects. Rather, it lists all the resources of the island for the attention of those concerned. Potential developments include the setting up and exploitation of predominantly-fulltime crofts, shell-fishing, and inshore white fishing, herring and offshore white fishing, forestry, tourism and holiday accommodation, minerals, peat utilisation, hill-land improvement, marine reclamation and seaweed resources. This list is significant and merits the attention of the Highlands & Islands Development Board.

Harris, on the other hand, presents possibilities on a much smaller and limited scale. However, there are expansion potentials in tweed, knitwear, and craft industries, with tourism promising to be a good base for the island's economy. As the age-structure of the crofting population changes, there will be a useful re-organisation and enlargement of existing holdings to make for better economic units. There could well be plants for fish meal and canning, working in conjunction with fish-farming ventures.

Perhaps one of the most significant events which have occurred was the formation in 1972 of the Lewis Development Fund Limited. The Company has the following aims:

1. To strengthen and expand the economy of Lewis and in consequence that of the Western Isles by promoting and encouraging the development of all the natural, economic and industrial resources of Lewis and the Western Isles.

2. To encourage the repopulation of the Western Isles and to encourage industries in the island to obtain the necessary staff and labour.

3. To encourage the building of shops, factories, public works, churches, places of amusement and any other works which the company might think fit.

4. To encourage tourism.

5. To promote and carry on businesses such as building, fishing, buying and selling, agriculture and manufacturing, etc.

The Company has given itself wide powers to lend and borrow money. A target of £150,000 is envisaged, which funds will then be used to help all kinds of economic and socio-economic ventures.

Surveys carried out in the Minch area in 1971 by British Petroleum and the Gas Council have indicated the possibility of oil. While there are no signs of the traditional anticlines—the dome-shaped geological structures—which normally signify the presence of commercial quantities of oil or gas, there are hopes for secondary sources in the more complicated rock-structures which could be oil-bearing. The sea-bed of the Minch is young rock of the type which bears oil in other parts of the world.

The assumption, in 1974, by the Western Isles Regional Authority of most of the functions of the mainland local authorities is thought by many to be a chance to sink or swim. Having been for so many decades under the thumb of external influences, the islands now are being given the opportunity to devise relevant methods for ensuring their socio-economic viability in the future.

All in all, the island is going through a period of re-stocking, to recover from the inhibiting influences of centuries-old history, economic isolation, and the ravages of two world wars. The emergent community, though smaller, will be as rich in quality and personal ideals as it has ever been. To say that of an island, of any island, indicates that its community is more than worthy of support in its endeavours to remain true to itself and its long-standing heritage of island life and living.

BIBLIOGRAPHY

Most of the world loves an island. Thus most of the world's island-groups have their own literature, mainly written by those attracted to islands as such, their motives sometimes rational, sometimes emotional, sometimes stemming merely from curiosity. For well on 1,000 years now, visitors drawn to the Hebrides have afterwards itched to curl their fingers round a pen of sorts to let others know of their discoveries, their feelings, their impressions and the nature of the land and the people they saw. The general public, too, has had a correspondingly avid, sometimes avuncular, interest in the life of these almost-last outposts of the European continent.

The bibliography for the island of Harris and Lewis is extensive : general articles of an informative and entertaining nature, official and personal reports and documents, novels, sketches, newspaper items (not always as accurate as they should be), topographical and social descriptions, and so on. These have fixed in perpetuity most aspects of life on the island, particularly from about 1750. Many items are of course out of print and available only in the older-established public libraries, in university libraries and in private collections of Highland books.

Some information about the island is in the form of unpublished manuscripts, and in books printed privately and with a limited circulation, published on the subscription system. Occasionally, certain oblique sources contain references to the isle folk, their way of life, and the conditions in which they lived and worked. These sources include, as might be expected, collections of verse in Gaelic and English by native authors, and folk-music and songs which reflect, often with startling clarity, the feelings and reactions of the people to the various social and economic burdens imposed on them by influences not always of their own making. The oral folktale and tradition field is yet another fruitful source of information, though a working knowledge of Gaelic is usually necessary to extract the essence.

AGRICULTURE AND FISHERIES FOR SCOTLAND, DEPARTMENT OF. *Scottish Peat Surveys*, Vol 2 : *Western Highlands and Islands.* Edinburgh, 1965

BIBLIOGRAPHY

ANCIENT MONUMENTS, ROYAL COMMISSION ON. *Ninth Report, with Inventory of Monuments and Constructions in the Outer Hebrides, Skye and the Small Isles.* HMSO, Edinburgh, 1928

ANDERSON, G. AND P. *Guide to the Highlands and Islands of Scotland.* Edinburgh, 1834

ANDERSON, J. *Account of the Present State of the Hebrides and West Coast of Scotland.* Edinburgh, 1785

ANSON, P. F. *Scots Fisherfolk.* Banff, 1950

ARGYLL, DUKE OF. *Crofts and Farms in the Hebrides.* Edinburgh, 1883

BADDELEY, M. J. B. *The Highlands of Scotland.* London, 1881

BADEN-POWELL, D. AND ELTON, C. *Raised Beach and Iron-age Midden in Lewis. Proc* Soc Antiq of Scot, Vol LXI, 1931-32

BEATON, A. J. *The Island of Lewis and its Fishermen-crofters.* London, 1878

BLACKIE, J. J. The Scottish Highlands and the Land Laws. London, 1885

BLAKE, J. L. 'Distribution of Surnames in Lewis.' *Scottish Studies,* Vol 10, 1966

BROWNE, J. *A History of the Highlands.* Glasgow, 1883

BUCHAN, A. *A Description of St Kilda.* Edinburgh, 1727

BUCHANAN, J. L. *Travels in the Western Hebrides.* London, 1793

BUCHANAN, R. *The Hebrid Isles.* London, 1883

BULLOCH, J. *The Life of the Celtic Church.* Edinburgh, 1963

CAIRD, J. B. and MOISLEY, H. A. 'Leadership and Innovation in the Crofting Communities of the Outer Hebrides.' *Sociological Review,* Vol 19, 1961

CAMPBELL, LORD COLIN. *The Crofter in History.* Edinburgh, 1886

CAMPBELL, M. S. *The Flora of Uig.* Arbroath, 1945

Conditions in the Highlands and Islands and Practicability of Relief by Emigration. Select Committee Report. Edinburgh, 1841

CONNELL, R. *St Kilda and the St Kildans.* London, 1887

CROFTERS COMMISSION. *Grazing and Agricultural Customs of the Outer Hebrides.* Report by A. Carmichael. Edinburgh, 1884

CROFTERS COMMISSION. *Minutes of Evidence.* Edinburgh, 1884

BIBLIOGRAPHY

CROFTERS COMMISSION COMMITTEE. *Report on the Social Condition of the People of Lewis in 1901 compared with Twenty Years Ago.* Edinburgh, 1902

CROWLEY, D. W. 'The Crofters' Party.' *Scot Hist Rev,* Vol 35. Edinburgh, 1956

CURWEN, E. C. 'The Hebrides—a Cultural Backwater.' *Antiquity,* 12. Gloucester, 1938

DARLING, F. FRASER. *West Highland Survey.* London, 1955

DARLING, F. FRASER. *Island Years.* London, 1940

DARLING, F. FRASER. *A Naturalist on Rona.* London, 1939

DARLING, F. FRASER. *Natural History in the Highlands and Islands.* London, 1947

DAY, J. P. *Public Administration in the Highlands and Islands.* London, 1918

DENDY, W. C. *The Wild Hebrides.* London, 1859

DILWORTH, REV DOM MARK. *Benedictine Monks of Ratisbon and Wurzburg in the 17th and 18th Centuries: Emigrés from the Highlands of Scotland. Trans* Gaelic Soc of Inverness, Vol XLIV, 1964-66

DONALDSON, G. *Northwards by Sea.* Edinburgh, 1966

DUCKWORTH, C. L. D. and LANGMUIR, G. E. *West Highland Steamers.* Prescot, 1967

DUNLOP, J. *The British Fisheries Society, 1786-1893.* Unpublished thesis (1952), Edinburgh University Library

ELLIOTT, J. S. 'St Kilda and the St Kildans.' *Journal* Birmingham Nat Hist & Phil Soc, 1, 1895

FEA, J. *The Fishermen in the Scottish Islands.* London, 1787

FEILDEN, H. W. *Journal of a Tour through the Outer Hebrides in 1870. Trans* Glasgow Nat Hist Soc, 11, 1870

FENTON, A. *Early and Traditional Cultivating Instruments in Scotland. Proc* Soc Antiq Scot, Vol XCVI, 1965

FISHERY BOARD FOR SCOTLAND. *Annual Reports and Statistics.* Edinburgh, 1887-1938

FRESSON, E. E. *Air Road to the Isles.* London, 1967

GAFFNEY, V. 'Summer Sheilings.' *Scot Hist Rev,* 38. Edinburgh, 1959

GEDDES, A. *The Isle of Lewis and Harris.* Edinburgh, 1955

BIBLIOGRAPHY

GEIKIE, J. 'The Long Island or Outer Hebrides.' *Good Words*, 1897

GIBSON, W. J. *Some Prehistoric Relics from Lewis. Proc* Soc Antiq Scot, Vol LXVIII, Edinburgh

GOODRICH-FREER, A. *The Outer Isles.* London, 1902

GORDON, S. 'Isles of the Outer Hebrides.' *Scot Geog Mag*, 57. Edinburgh, 1941

GORDON-CUMMING, C. F. *In the Hebrides.* London, 1883

GRAY, M. 'The Kelp Industry in the Highlands and Islands.' *Econ Hist Rev*, 2nd series, IV, No 2, 1951

GREGORY, D. *History of the Western Highlands and Islands of Scotland.* Edinburgh, 1836

HARVIE-BROWN, J. A. and BUCKLEY, T. E. *Vertebrate Fauna of the Outer Hebrides.* Edinburgh, 1889

HEATHCOTE, J. N. *St Kilda.* London, 1900

HIGHET, J. *The Scottish Churches.* London, 1960

HIGHLANDS AND ISLANDS COMMISSION. *Report.* Edinburgh, 1895

HIGHLANDS AND ISLANDS DEVELOPMENT BOARD. *Annual Reports.* Inverness, in progress

JAATINEN, S. 'The Human Geography of the Outer Hebrides.' *Acta Geographica*, 16, No 2, Helsinki, 1957

JAMESON, R. *Mineralogy of the Scottish Isles.* Edinburgh, 1800

JEHU, T. and CRAIG, R. M. *The Geology of the Outer Hebrides. Trans* Royal Soc Edin, Vols 53-7

LACAILLE, A. D. *Stone Industry at Valtos, Uig, Lewis. Proc* Soc Antiq Scot, Vol LXXI, 1936-7

LEWIS ASSOCIATION. *Reports 1-7: General Economic Survey of the Island; Town and Country Planning; the Harris Tweed Industry; External and Internal Transport; the Fishing Industry; Health.* Stornoway, 1944-54

LEYDEN, J. *Tour in the Highlands and Western Islands.* Edinburgh, 1903

MACANDREW, H. 'The Highlands and Islands; Social and Literary History.' *Celtic Magazine*, XI, 1886

MACARTHUR, McCRONE and McHAFFIE. *Steamers of the Clyde and Western Isles.* Motherwell, 1965

MacAskill, A. J. *Differences in Dialect, Vocabulary, and General Idiom between the Islands*. Trans Gaelic Soc Inverness, Vol XLIII, 1960-63

MacAulay, K. *Voyage to St Kilda*. London, 1764

MacBrayne, D., Limited. *A Hundred Years of Progress*. Mac-Brayne Centenary, 1851-1951. Glasgow, 1951

MacCuish, D. J. *The Origin and Development of Crofting Law*. Trans Gaelic Soc Inverness, Vol XLIII, 1960-63

MacCulloch, J. *Description of the Western Islands*. London, 1824

MacDonald, D. *Tales and Traditions of the Lews*. Stornoway, 1967

MacDonald, J. *General View of the Agriculture of the Hebrides*. Edinburgh, 1811

MacFarlane, J. *The 'Men' in the Lews*. Stornoway, 1924

MacIver, D. *Placenames of Lewis and Harris*. Stornoway, 1934

MacKenzie, H. R. *Yachting and Electioneering in the Hebrides*. Inverness, 1886

MacKenzie, K. S. *An Economical History of the Hebrides or Western Islands of Scotland*. Trans Gaelic Soc Inverness, Vol XXIV, 1899-1901

MacKenzie, W. *Gaelic Incantations, Charms and Blessings of the Hebrides*. Inverness, 1895

MacKenzie, W. C. *History of the Outer Hebrides*. Paisley, 1903

MacKenzie, W. C. *Short History of the Highlands of Scotland*. Paisley, 1907

MacKenzie, W. C. *The Book of the Lews*. Paisley, 1919

MacKenzie, W. C. *The Western Isles*. Paisley, 1932

MacKenzie, W. C. *Colonel Colin MacKenzie*. Edinburgh, 1952

MacLean, L. *Sketches of the Island of St Kilda*. Glasgow, 1838

MacLeod, M. *Gaelic in Highland Education*. Trans Gaelic Society Inverness, Vol XLIII, 1960-63

MacRae, A. *Revivals in the Highlands and Islands in the 19th Century*. Stirling, 1906

Malcolm, G. *The Population, Crofts, Sheep-Walks and Deer Forests of the Highlands and Islands*. Edinburgh, 1883

Martin, M. *A Late Voyage to St Kilda*. London, 1698. Also Stirling, 1934

BIBLIOGRAPHY

MARTIN, M. *Description of the Western Islands of Scotland*. London, 1705. Also Glasgow, 1884

MILLER, H. *A Summer Ramble Among the Hebrides*. Edinburgh, 1858

MILLINGTON, R. *The Islanders*. London, 1966

MOISLEY, H. A. 'Harris Tweed : A Growing Highland Industry.' *Economic Geography*, Vol 37, 1961

MOISLEY, H. A. 'The Deserted Hebrides.' *Scottish Studies*, Vol 10, 1966

MONRO, D. 'A Description of the Western Isles of Scotland called Hybrides, c 1549.' Stirling, 1934

MORGAN, J. E. 'The Diseases of St Kilda.' *Brit & Foreign Med & Chir Review*, XXIX, 1862

MORISON, D. *Ceol-Mara—Songs from the Isle of Lewis*. London, 1935

MORISONE, J. 'Description of the Lews.' *Spottiswode Miscellany*, Vol 2, Edinburgh, 1845

MORRISON, A. *The Contullish Papers, 1706-1720. Trans* Gaelic Soc Inverness, Vol XLIV, 1964-6

NEW STATISTICAL ACCOUNT OF SCOTLAND. Edinburgh, 1840-5

NICHOLSON, A. *Report on the State of Education in the Hebrides*. Edinburgh, 1866

NICHOLSON, N. *Lord of the Isles*. London, 1955

O'DELL, A. C. and WALTON, K. *The Highlands and Islands of Scotland*. London, 1960

Old Statistical Account of Scotland. Edinburgh, 1796

Reports and Correspondence on the Subject of Wrecking in the Hebrides. (Parliamentary Papers). London, 1867

Report on the State of Education in the Hebrides. (Parliamentary Papers). London, 1867

SCOTT, W. R. *Report to the Board of Agriculture on Home Industries in the Highlands and Islands*. (Parliamentary Paper.) Edinburgh, 1914

SCOTTISH ECONOMIC COMMITTEE. *Report on the Highlands and Islands*. Edinburgh, 1938

SCOTTISH MOUNTAINEERING CLUB. *The Islands of Scotland*. Edinburgh, 1934

SETON, G. *St Kilda—Past and Present.* Edinburgh, 1878

SINCLAIR, C. *Thatched Houses.* Edinburgh, 1953

SINCLAIR, SIR J. (ed). *The [Old] Statistical Account of Scotland drawn up from the Communication of the Ministers of the Parishes.* 21 Vols. Edinburgh, 1791-9

SMITH, A. *Lewisiana, or Life in the Outer Hebrides.* London, 1875

SMITH, P. G. A. *The Romance of Harris.* Edinburgh, 1914

ST-FOND, B. F. *Voyage en Angleterre, en Ecosse, et aux Isles Hebrides.* Paris, 1797. Translated London, 1799. Also Glasgow, 1907

STEPHEN, R. M. *Glimpses of Portrona.* Stornoway, nd.

STEVEN, A. 'The Human Geography of Lewis.' *Scot Geog Mag,* 41, Edinburgh, 1925

STEWART, M. *Ronay.* Oxford, 1933

THOMAS, F. W. L. *Notice of Beehive Houses in Harris; with Traditions of the Water-horse connected therewith. Proc* Soc Antiq Scot, Vol III, 1862

THOMAS, F. W. L. *On the Primeval Dwellings and Hypogea of the Outer Hebrides. Proc* Soc Antiq Scot, Vol VII, 1866

THOMPSON, F. G. *Harris Tweed: The Story of an Island Industry.* Newton Abbot, 1969

THOMPSON, R. *Cruise in the Western Hebrides.* Glasgow, 1891

WALKER, J. *Harris in 1765. Trans* Gaelic Soc Inverness, Vol XXIV, 1900

WEDDERSPOON, T. *Island of Bernera, Harris. Trans* Inverness Field Club. Vol VII, 1909

WESTEPN HIGHLANDS AND ISLANDS COMMISSION. *Reports.* Edinburgh, 1890-91

WHITTET, M. 'Problems of Psychiatry in the Highlands and Islands.' *Scottish Medical Journal,* Vol 8, No 8, 1963

207

ADDENDA

MacIver, R. M. *As A Tale that is Told*. Chicago, 1968

Thompson, Francis. *St Kilda and other Hebridean Outliers*. Newton Abbot, 1970

Mitchell, Joseph. *Reminiscences of my Life in the Highlands*. 2 Vols, reprinted 1971, Newton Abbot

Dougal, J. Wilson. *Island Memories*. Edinburgh, 1937

Jamieson, A. M. *The Old Lewis Guard*. Stornoway, nd(c1910)

Swire, Otta. *The Outer Hebrides and their Legends*. Edinburgh, 1966

ACKNOWLEDGMENTS

I have to acknowledge the valuable help of many people in the completion of this book. Some aided by the mere mention of a fruitful source of information. Others, such as the officials of the various Government offices I contacted, went to much trouble to unearth, and present in excellent form, facts and figures not otherwise available to me as a private individual. The *Stornoway Gazette* has been more than helpful in making its files and office facilities available for research. And Mr I. R. MacKay of Inverness did me the kindness of reading through my draft manuscript and commenting on those errors and omissions which would have detracted from the final script. Any mistakes and inconsistencies which remain are to be laid at my door.

INDEX

Page numbers in italic indicate illustrations

INDEX